A Field Guide to Seashores Coloring Book

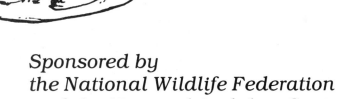

John C. Kricher

Illustrations by Gordon Morrison

Roger Tory Peterson, Consulting Editor

*Sponsored by
the National Wildlife Federation
and the National Audubon Society*

Houghton Mifflin Company   Boston   1989

To Aimée and Suzanne,
for all the shores
we have traveled together
and those that are yet to come.

Introduction copyright © 1989 by
   Roger Tory Peterson
Text copyright © 1989 by
   John C. Kricher
Illustrations copyright © 1989 by
   Gordon Morrison

Printed in the United States of America

J 10 9 8 7 6 5 4 3 2 1

Introduction

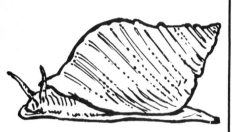

Exploring seashores, those unique areas where land meets ocean, is a visual activity, a game or sport that trains the eye. Most budding naturalists soon acquire a copy of one or more of the Field Guides, such as *A Field Guide to the Atlantic Seashore, A Field Guide to Southeastern and Caribbean Seashores,* or others that specialize in plants, fish, or birds. These handy, pocket-sized books offer shortcuts to identification, reducing things to basic shapes and patterns, with arrows pointing to the special "field marks" by which one species can be separated from another.

Although even a person who is colorblind can become skilled at identifying birds by their patterns, or shells by their shapes, for most of us color is the first clue. This coloring book, skillfully written by John C. Kricher, will sharpen your observations and condition your memory for the days you spend along the seashore. By beachcombing during the day and filling in the colors during evening hours, you will be better informed about the impressive diversity of plants and animals that share seashores with vacationing people. Armed with binoculars for spotting birds, and a pail and shovel for digging worms, shellfish, and arthropods, you can use this guide to identify and learn about many of our most common seashore inhabitants.

A coloring book such as this will help your color perception, but it will not teach you to draw, unless you copy the basic line drawings so artfully prepared by Gordon Morrison. You might try to sketch things in the field, if only roughly in pencil.

Exploring seashores, whether along the Atlantic, Pacific, or Gulf coasts, can be many things — an art, a science, a game, or a sport — but above all it is an absorbing activity that sharpens the senses, especially the eye. If you draw or paint, the sense of touch also comes into play; the images of the eye and the mind are transferred by hand to paper. In the process, you become more aware of the natural world — the real world — and inevitably you become an environmentalist.

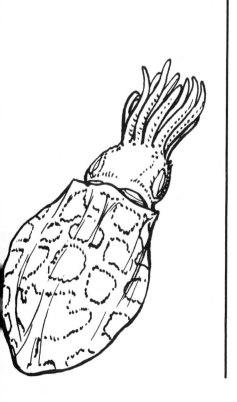

Most of you may find colored pencils best suited for coloring this book, but if you are handy with brushes and paints, you may prefer to fill in the outlines with watercolors. Crayons, too, can be used. But don't labor; have fun. That is what beachcombing and this coloring book are all about.

Roger Tory Peterson

About This Book

Like *A Field Guide to Forests Coloring Book*, this book concentrates on habitats — the places where animals live — rather than on a particular group of plants or animals. *A Field Guide to Seashores Coloring Book* begins with the rocky shores of New England. It continues on to the sandy beaches and coastal seas of the Southeast and Gulf of Mexico, with a look at the mangroves and coral reefs of Florida and the Caribbean, and ends with the rugged shores and kelp forests of the Pacific Coast. Each coastal habitat is home to an interesting combination of plants and animals. The vast deep oceans cover 71 percent of the earth's surface. By coloring the drawings in this book, you will become introduced to some of the most fascinating forms of life on the planet.

This book is meant to be a field guide as well as a coloring book. You will be able to use the book in the field to identify many common plants and animals along the seashores. By coloring pictures of them, you will enhance your powers of observation and ability to see detail. In short, you will not only create for yourself a personalized and beautiful volume, but you'll sharpen your senses as an observer of nature. I think you will agree that the splendid drawings of Gordon Morrison cry out to be colored. Although the colored drawings on the endpapers and my comments in the text can serve as your guides in selecting colors, we encourage you to use your own eyes as well. Many marine animals are variable in color. We illustrate the most common color patterns, but you may see something different. It's your book: color things the way you see them.

Our coastal environments are among our most precious resources. They are also among our most fragile environments. Threatened by pressures to develop more land for houses and commercial buildings, and by pollution from both land and sea, seashores are often not valued or appreciated as natural habitats until it is too late. Barrier beaches protect bays and coastlines from the effects of storms and serve as refuges for many migrating bird species. Salt marshes and mangrove swamps provide valuable nutrients that sustain oceanic life, including some of our most important game birds, sport fishes, commercial fishes, and shellfish. Estuaries — places where fresh and salt water mix — serve as nurseries for vast numbers of fishes. Seashores also have immense esthetic value. We travel to the beach not only to enjoy bathing in the surf, but to beachcomb and get a glimpse of life in the oceans. What kind of crab is that? What are those birds diving in the waves? What kind of seaweed is that? What kind of fish did that angler just haul in? When you learn to identify some of the plants and animals, you begin to ask how they live and interact together. Soon you be-

gin to realize that the whole is more than the sum of its parts. You become an environmentalist.

It is our hope that this little book will help you better understand and appreciate our seashores, and that you will contribute to their preservation and protection.

John C. Kricher

How to Use This Book

Seashores. The seashore is the place where land meets ocean. It is often a harsh environment, where plants and animals must cope with salt spray, winds, pounding waves, and shifting sands. At the same time, however, it presents many opportunities for organisms to thrive. Rivers carry sediments rich in nutrients, and deposit them in bays, estuaries, and salt marshes. Sunlit shallow coastal waters provide ideal conditions for the growth of seaweeds and tiny plants called phytoplankton. These plants form the base of the marine coastal food chains that sustain fishes, marine mammals, seabirds, and crustaceans (crabs, shrimps, and their relatives), including all the creatures that provide delicious meals for seafood lovers. Rocks, piers, and pilings serve as places where many kinds of plants and animals can attach themselves. As you wander along seashores, take note of the many ways plants and animals are adapted, both to make their livings and to survive the rigors of this narrow space between land and sea. Crabs and worms burrow, for example, and mollusks (snails, clams, and other animals that live inside shells) can open or close their shells.

Intertidal zone. Perhaps the most noticeable and distinctive feature of seashores is the rhythmic motion of the tides. Caused by the position of the moon in relation to the sun, tides are variable but nonetheless predictable. Many organisms live between the points of high tide and low tide, an area called the **intertidal zone.** When the tide is in (at high tide), these organisms are able to feed on food brought by the rich coastal waters. As the waves recede, waste products are washed out to sea, and eggs and larvae (young shellfish, fishes, or mollusks) are dispersed by the sea to colonize other areas. However, when the tide is out (at low tide), these creatures, which require salt water, are forced to "shut down" and wait it out until the next high tide. Beachcombing is quite rewarding during low tide. You can poke among the seaweeds and see all manner of animals tucked in to remain moist. Rock crevices also provide shelter during low tide, as do tidepools, depressions in rocks that hold salt water when the tide is out. Barnacles, mussels, and many other animals are attached to rocks or pilings, and they often close up their shells when exposed to air. Because plants and animals differ in their abilities to tolerate exposure to air, the intertidal zone is usually subdivided into a series of zones. As you pass from low-water line to high-water line, you'll notice a zone of brown algae, a zone of blue mussels, a barnacle zone, and perhaps a zone of green algae. The order of the plants and animals may change from one part of the coastline to the next. If you enjoy putting on a mask and snorkel, high tide is ideal for looking at the intertidal zone.

Seashore habitats.   As you travel about our country's coastlines, you cannot help but notice the diversity of seashore habitats. Rocky coasts characterize both the northeastern and northwestern coasts. To the southeast, southwest, and along the Gulf Coast, sandy beaches prevail. The southern tip of Florida, the West Indies, and the Caribbean islands have mangrove swamps and coral reefs. Within any major region there is also considerable variety. Barrier beaches, which themselves are habitat for many plants and animals, protect salt marshes, which support their own plant and animal communities. Oysters and mussels grow in vast beds, providing habitat for dozens of creatures that live on their shells. Many marine plants and animals need to attach themselves to some solid object like a shell, rock, or dock. Many attach themselves to the bottoms of boats, to the distress of the boat owners. Look at the pattern of zonation on dock pilings from the low- to the high-water mark. Inspect shells and driftwood washed up from the sea for odd creatures attached. Beachcombing is fun no matter what the season. Summer is fine for sun worshippers, but winter storms may wash many oddities of the sea ashore. Put on warm clothes and brave the winds.

Kinds of plants.   Many terrestrial plants are adapted to withstand salt spray and evaporation caused by offshore winds. Botanizing on sand dunes or a salt marsh is an ideal way to become acquainted with these species. Everyone who goes to the seashore has seen various kinds of "seaweed." These plants, called algae, are quite different from terrestrial (land-dwelling) plants. They must remain moist or they will perish. All algae lack the stiff tissues of terrestrial plants; ocean currents suspend them in the water, often in long strands. They grow rapidly and take energy from the sun in a manner virtually identical to that of terrestrial plants. Some groups of marine plants, called phytoplankton, are not visible to the naked eye but must be seen through a microscope. These tiny plants are often called the "grasses of the sea." They feed and thus support a network of animals in the ocean. In this book we'll look at examples of seashore plants, seaweeds (algae), and phytoplankton.

Kinds of animals. Marine animals fall into several major groups:

Coelenterates. These are the jellyfish, sea anemones, corals, and hydroids, such as the Portuguese Man-of-War. Many wash up on beaches or invade shallow bays. Anemones attach themselves to rocks and pilings. Corals form vast reefs in tropical waters.

Segmented worms. Many kinds of worms burrow in sand or mud along shore. These creatures range from active graceful swimmers to odd-looking tube-dwellers that sweep the mud with moplike tentacles. A few other worms, not segmented, also live in the sea.

Mollusks. These are the snails, clams, mussels, squids, octopuses, and chitons. Some snails are predaceous, feeding on clams, barnacles, oysters, and mussels. Others are herbivores, grazing like diminutive marine cows on tiny algae that grow on rock surfaces. Chitons (see p. 63) also graze on plants and are well adapted for holding fast to rocks, enduring the heaviest waves. Clams and mussels stay put, filtering the water, extracting oxygen and food. Squids and octopuses swim actively, using their own version of jet propulsion to flee from predators or find food.

Arthropods. The word *arthropod* means "joint-legged." If you look at crabs, lobsters, and shrimps, you will see that their legs are jointed, as in their distant relatives, the insects and spiders. Arthropods also have an external skeleton, which must be shed at intervals so the animal can grow. In the sea, the crustaceans are the predominant group of arthropods. They include the shrimps, lobsters, crabs, barnacles, amphipods, isopods, and copepods.

Echinoderms. Echinoderms are spiny-skinned animals. This group includes the sea stars (starfish), brittle stars, and sea urchins, as well as the sea cucumbers.

Tunicates. These are baglike creatures that filter water to extract food and oxygen, much as clams do. However, their larvae (young) are tadpole-like and are thus very similar to tiny fishes, with gills, a stiff "backbone," and a nerve cord.

Vertebrates. These are animals with backbones. They include the bony fishes, sharks and rays, sea turtles, marine mammals, and seabirds. Because of their large size, they are among the most commonly noticed marine animals. We'll meet many of them in this book.

Now that you know what you might find, let's beachcomb.

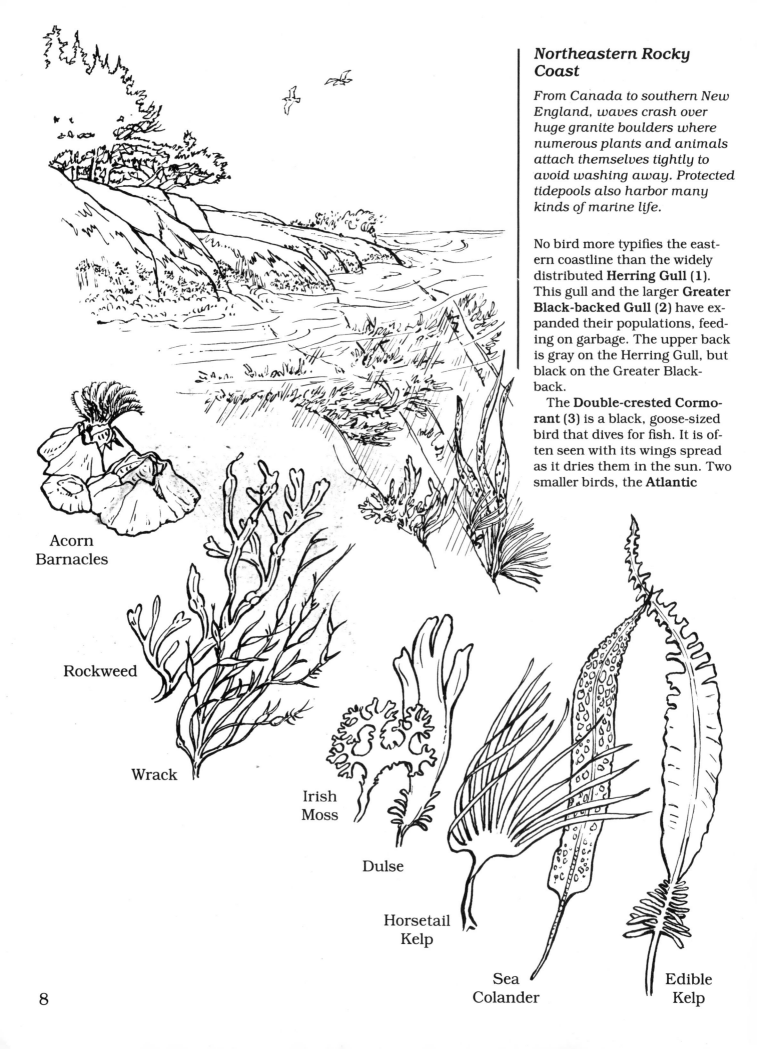

Northeastern Rocky Coast

From Canada to southern New England, waves crash over huge granite boulders where numerous plants and animals attach themselves tightly to avoid washing away. Protected tidepools also harbor many kinds of marine life.

No bird more typifies the eastern coastline than the widely distributed **Herring Gull (1)**. This gull and the larger **Greater Black-backed Gull (2)** have expanded their populations, feeding on garbage. The upper back is gray on the Herring Gull, but black on the Greater Blackback.

The **Double-crested Cormorant (3)** is a black, goose-sized bird that dives for fish. It is often seen with its wings spread as it dries them in the sun. Two smaller birds, the **Atlantic**

Acorn
Barnacles

Rockweed

Wrack

Irish
Moss

Dulse

Horsetail
Kelp

Sea
Colander

Edible
Kelp

Puffin (4) and the **Black Guillemot** (5), also dive for fish. Atlantic Puffins have been reintroduced to some islands off Maine. The guillemot breeds along the coast from Maine northward.

A look at the rocks reveals different zones between the low- and high-tide lines. Each zone is home to a different group of marine plants and animals, depending on the amount of exposure they can tolerate during low tide. High on the rocks is the **barnacle zone**, where white **Acorn Barnacles** (6) are attached in dense populations. Each barnacle is permanently housed in a small crater of its own making, and once it settles, it can never move from its point of attachment. Barnacles are crustaceans. They feed by waving their jointed, netlike legs in the water, entrapping tiny marine organisms called plankton (see p. 40). When the tide is out, the barnacle tightly closes its shell, a protection against drying. Beneath the barnacle zone is the **rockweed zone**, where thick clumps of slick algae called **Rockweed** (7) and **Wrack** (8) are attached. These plants, which are golden brown in color, have small bladders that help the plant both to float and to absorb the pounding of the waves. The two lowest zones, the **Irish moss zone** and the **kelp zone**, are exposed only when the tide is very low. **Irish Moss** (9) is normally deep purple-red, though it may look quite green because it contains chlorophyll. Similar in color but larger is **Dulse** (10). **Kelp** includes several species of large algae, all of which are brown. **Horsetail Kelp** (11) has a wide frond with many fingerlike strands. **Sea Colander** (12) is rather like "Swiss cheese," with numerous holes. **Edible Kelp** (13) has a very long frond with deep lobes. The holes and lobes help these kelps avoid being damaged by waves.

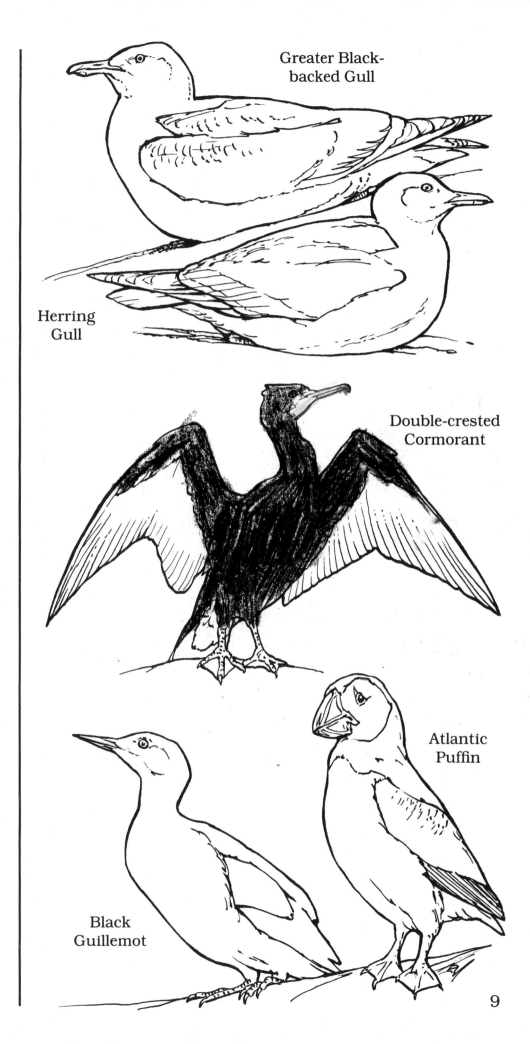

Greater Black-backed Gull

Herring Gull

Double-crested Cormorant

Atlantic Puffin

Black Guillemot

9

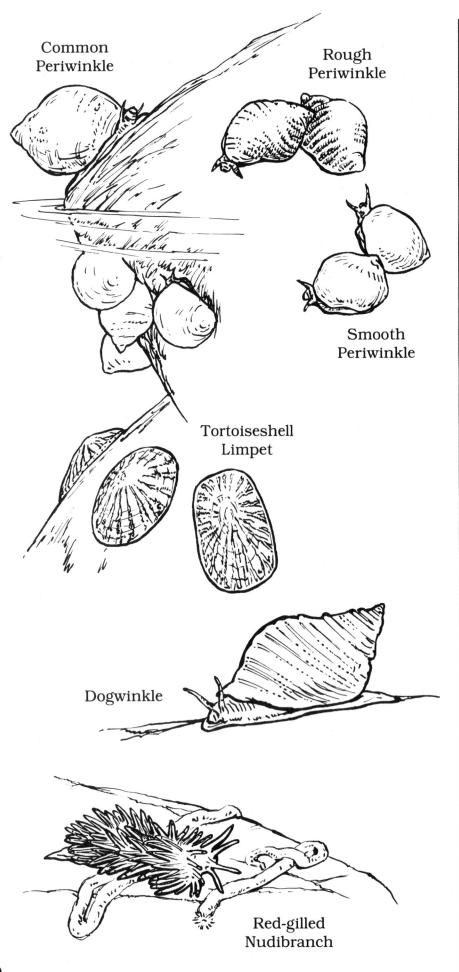

Common
Periwinkle

Rough
Periwinkle

Smooth
Periwinkle

Tortoiseshell
Limpet

Dogwinkle

Red-gilled
Nudibranch

Rocky Intertidal Snails

Three kinds of small snails called periwinkles are found throughout the rocky intertidal zone. The **Common Periwinkle (14)** is the most abundant, and also the largest. It spread to North America from Europe. The **Rough Periwinkle (15)** is similar but has tiny grooves in its shell. The **Smooth Periwinkle (16)** is often bright orange or yellow, the most colorful of the three. All eat algae.

The shape of the **Tortoiseshell Limpet (17)** allows it to cling tightly to the rock face and tolerate wave pounding without washing away. The ornate brown and white patterning, plus the shape, gives the animal its name "tortoiseshell." Limpets eat algae.

The **Dogwinkle (18)** is variable in color. Most Dogwinkles are white, but some are yellow, orange, brown, or white with brown banding. They devour both barnacles and mussels, boring into them with a raspy tongue.

Red-gilled Nudibranchs (19) are snails that lack shells. The name *nudibranch* means "naked gills," a reference to the many clublike protrusions, called cerata, that are used for respiration but are not protected by a shell. This species is found low in the intertidal zone, feeding on hydroids (see p. 17).

Rocky Intertidal Echinoderms

Sea stars, also known as "starfish," are predators. They feed on clams and mussels, which they open by patiently pulling the shell apart using suction from their numerous tube feet. The sea star then slides its stomach into the opened mollusk and digests it! **Forbes' Asterias (20)**, shown here, is rufous with an orange spot. This spot, the madreporite, controls the flow of water in and out of the animal's body, providing suction for the tube feet.

Blood stars (21), as the name implies, are usually bright red, though some may be orange or yellow. Look for them in tidepools, where they feed on sponges.

Although the **Green Sea Urchin (22)** resembles a prickly ball, its spines are quite blunt and it is easy to pick up. This olive-green creature feeds on algae, which it scrapes off rocks. Its tube feet help it hang on the rock face during the heaviest waves.

The **Orange-footed Sea Cucumber (23)** is slaty gray to reddish purple, with orange tube feet. It captures tiny animals with its bushy tentacles.

The spectacular **Basket Star (24)** is mostly a deepwater animal, though some wash into the intertidal zone. Each of the five arms has many branches, and may be up to 18 inches long. Some Basket Stars are yellow, some cream, some rich brown. They feed on worms and clams.

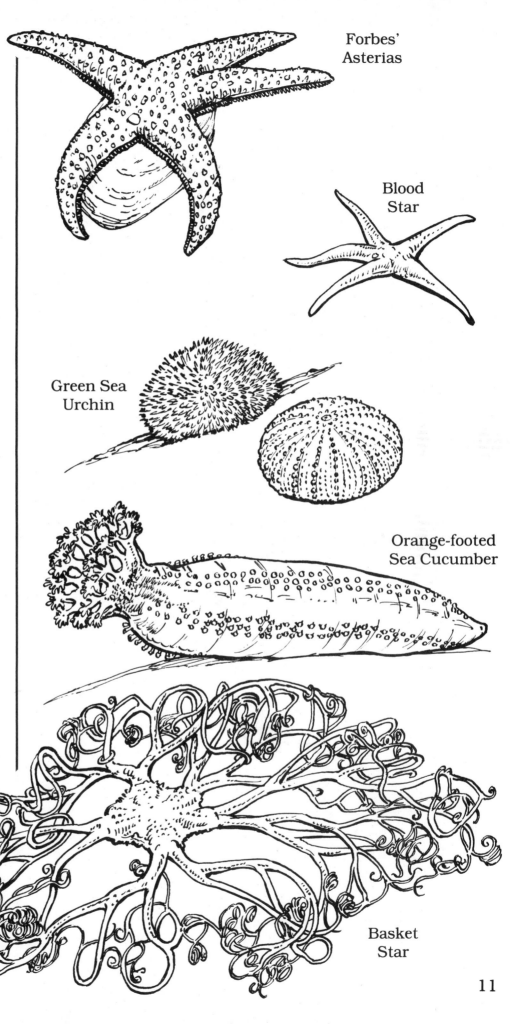

Forbes' Asterias

Blood Star

Green Sea Urchin

Orange-footed Sea Cucumber

Basket Star

11

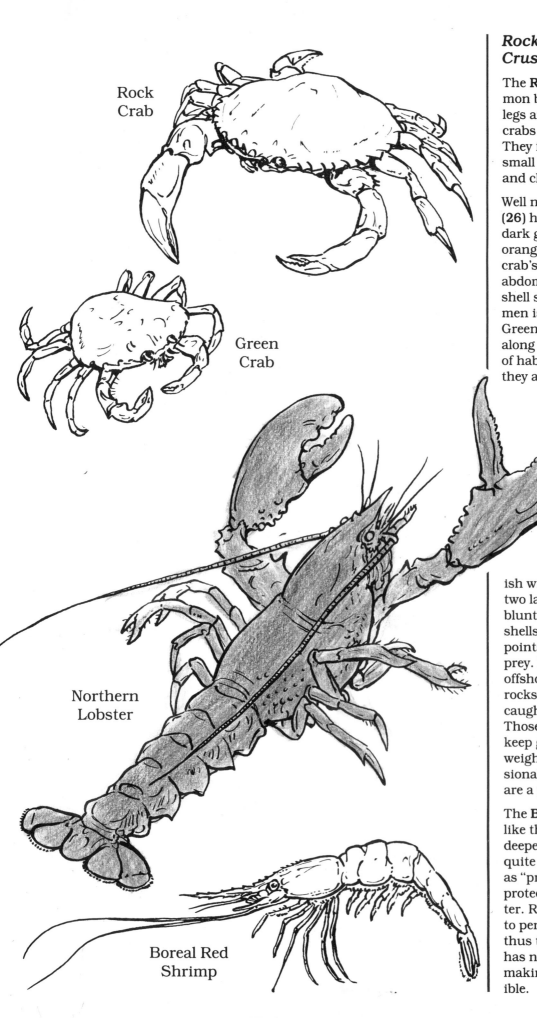

Rock
Crab

Green
Crab

Northern
Lobster

Boreal Red
Shrimp

Rocky Shore Crustaceans

The **Rock Crab (25)** is cinnamon brown, with pale orange legs and claws. Look for rock crabs in crevices or tidepools. They feed on dead fishes and small invertebrates like worms and clams.

Well named, the **Green Crab (26)** has a light green shell with dark green blotches, and is pale orange on its underside. A crab's underside is actually its abdomen, tucked under the shell so that the tip of the abdomen is near the crab's mouth! Green crabs are common all along the coast in many kinds of habitats. Like most crabs, they are scavengers.

Most famous as a bright red table delicacy, the **Northern Lobster (27)** is normally greenish with orange patches. The two large claws differ: one has blunt tubercles for crushing shells, the other has sharp points for pinching and holding prey. Lobsters are found mostly offshore, where they live among rocks and in crevices. They are caught in baited lobster traps. Those that escape the traps keep growing; some giants can weigh over 40 pounds. Occasional lobsters are caught that are a pale blue in color!

The **Boreal Red Shrimp (28)**, like the lobster, is partial to deeper waters. Red shrimp are quite edible and are often served as "prawns." The red color helps protect the shrimp in deep water. Red wavelengths of light fail to penetrate into deep water, thus the red color of the animal has no light to reflect from it, making the animal nearly invisible.

Offshore Birds and Mammals

During winter large numbers of **Common Loons (29)** and **Horned Grebes (30)** can be found diving in the shallow ocean along the shoreline. The loon is a gooze-sized bird that is gray when in winter plumage. It has a pale bill. The grebe is the size of a small duck, with a grayish black back and a white neck and underside. Its face is white and its head is black. The eyes are bright red. Loons and grebes feed on fish.

The **Common Eider (31)** is a large oceanic duck that dives for mussels and clams. Males are boldly patterned in black and white, with a greenish yellow bill. Females are grayish brown. Many hundreds of eiders may flock together on the ocean, in groups known as "rafts."

The **Harbor Seal (32)** is commonly spotted reclining atop an exposed rock. Sometimes it can be seen submerged, with only its head or even just its nose out of water. Harbor seals are fast swimmers and feed on fish.

Standing along the rocky shore, it is sometimes possible to spot whale spouts offshore. The whale's spout is its exhaled breath: though totally oceanic, whales are mammals and must surface to breathe air just as we do. The **Fin Whale (33)**, which can reach a length of 60 feet, is among the larger whales. It feeds by capturing small fishes and invertebrates in its filterlike mouth, which is lined with horny material called baleen. The baleen helps trap the animals, which are often tiny.

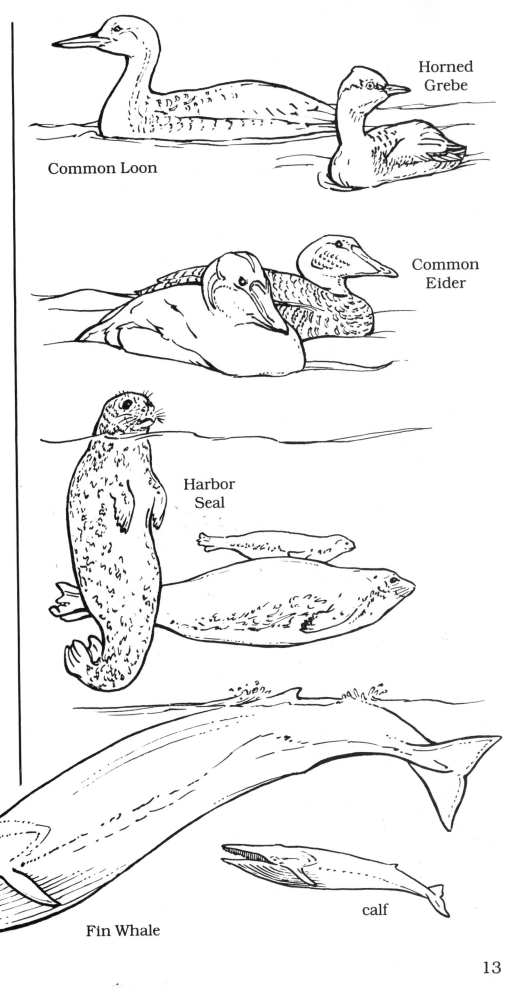

Horned Grebe

Common Loon

Common Eider

Harbor Seal

Fin Whale

calf

13

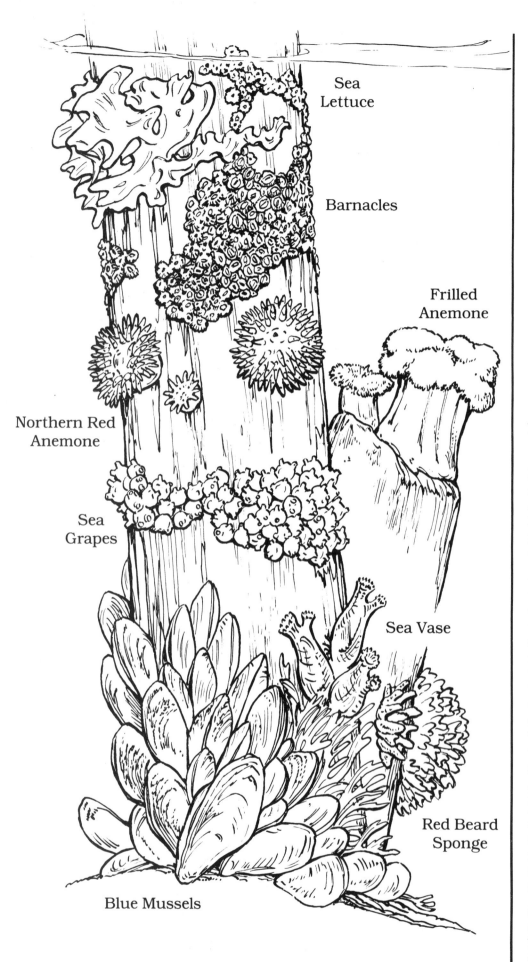

Sea
Lettuce

Barnacles

Frilled
Anemone

Northern Red
Anemone

Sea
Grapes

Sea Vase

Red Beard
Sponge

Blue Mussels

A Dock Piling

A close inspection of a dock piling at low tide will reveal how many kinds of marine plants and animals make their homes here. Like the rocks, pilings show patterns of zonation, though most animals are found lowest on the piling, where they are under water most of the time.

Sea Lettuce (34) is a bright green algae that is often attached near the high-tide mark, in the barnacle zone. It is also seen frequently in tidepools.

Though anemones resemble plants when open, they are coelenterates — animals related to jellyfish. When exposed, anemones contract their tentacle ring and resemble blobs of jelly. The flowerlike tentacle ring contains hundreds of stinging cells, used to capture food. The **Frilled Anemone (35)** is common; it has white tentacles atop a brownish red stalk. The **Northern Red Anemone (36)** is reddish green with red tentacles.

Sea squirts are baglike animals that attach themselves to a rock or piling. Water enters through one of two openings, called siphons, and exits through the other. As the water passes through the body, gills filter out tiny plankton for food. **Sea Grapes (37)** are common sea squirts. They are yellow-brown. The **Sea Vase (38)** is mostly transparent white, with yellow around the siphon tubes.

Blue Mussels (39) often grow in huge numbers, covering rocks and pilings. These mussels filter water and remove plankton for food. Mussels attach themselves to things by making very strong threads.

Red Beard Sponge (40) often encrusts pilings. Its many bright red branches all filter water, extracting tiny plankton.

14

Rocky Coast Fishes

The **Atlantic Cod (41)**, like the lobster, is one of the staple foods of New Englanders. These fish, which can approach 6 feet in length, are caught in large schools offshore, on fishing grounds such as Georges Bank and the Grand Banks. Cod vary in color: most are greenish yellow but some are reddish.

Sand Lances (42) are pencil-shaped fish only 4 to 6 inches in length. They are found in large schools just offshore and serve as important food for seabirds, fin whales, humpbacks, and porpoises. Color varies, but these fish are usually bluish or olive-brown with silvery undersides.

The **Tautog (43)** is a stout fish that can grow to 3 feet in length. It feeds on mussels and crabs, which it crushes with its strong jaws and teeth. Most Tautogs are grayish brown and greenish, with dark blotches. Tautogs inhabit rocky shores, breakwaters, ledges, and wrecks.

Redfish (44), which grow to a length of almost 2 feet, live over rocky bottoms in shallow to deep water. They range in color from orange to bright red, with large black eyes. Like bass, they have sharp spines on the dorsal fin that runs along the upper back. Redfish eat mostly shrimps and other crustaceans, as well as small fishes.

The **Goosefish (45)** has a huge head and a wide mouth studded with sharp teeth. The long head spine has a lure used to bring small fish close enough to capture. Goosefish grow to a length of 4 feet and can weigh up to 50 pounds. You can often find them in shallow water along the tide line, but they inhabit deep water as well. This fish is brownish black on top with scattered white spots, and white underneath.

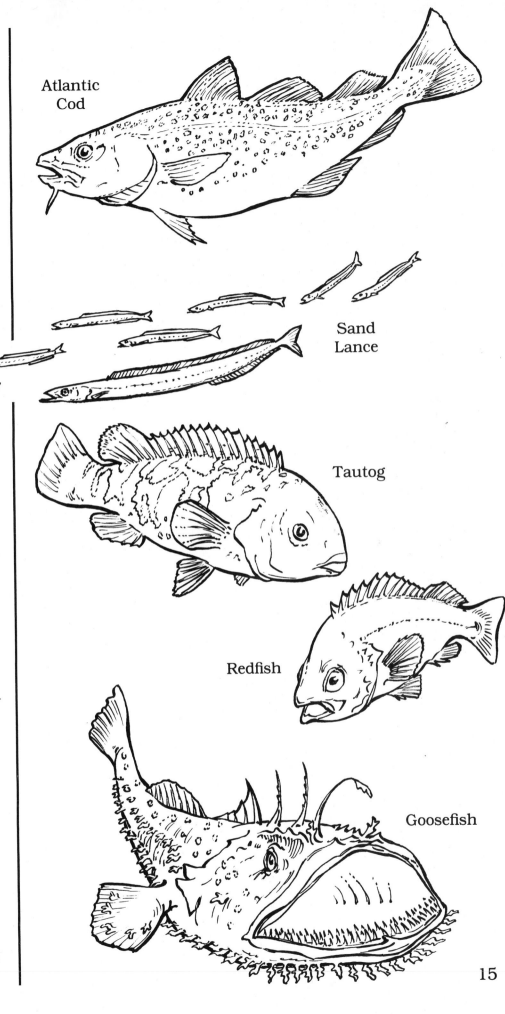

Atlantic Cod

Sand Lance

Tautog

Redfish

Goosefish

15

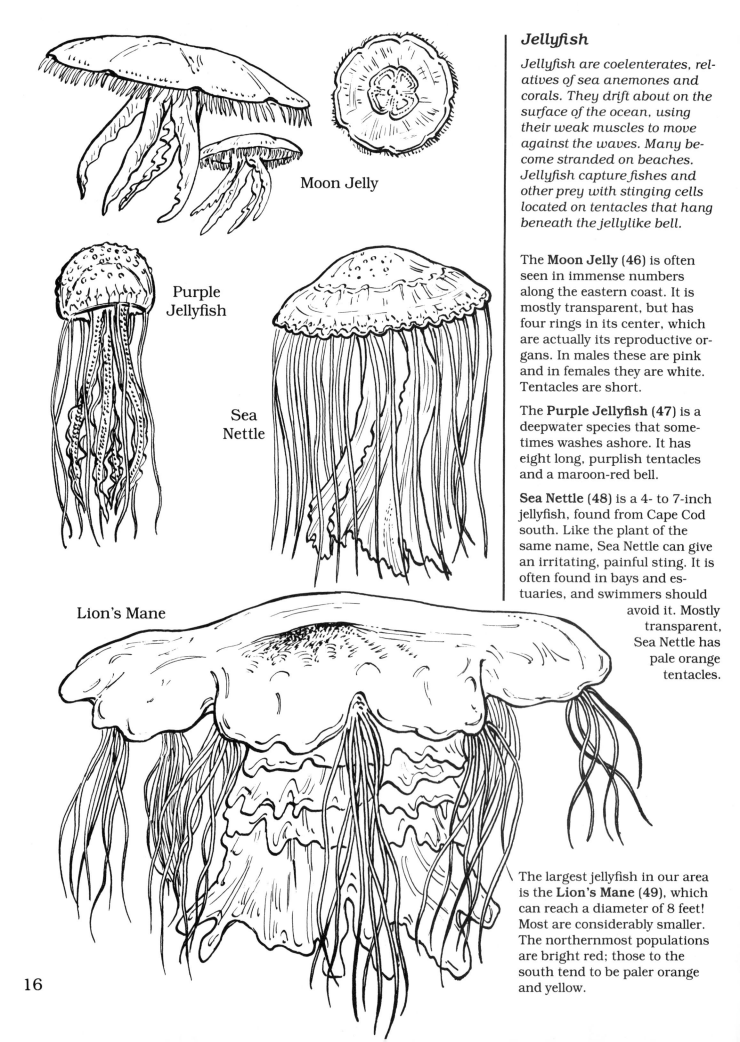

Moon Jelly

Purple Jellyfish

Sea Nettle

Lion's Mane

Jellyfish

Jellyfish are coelenterates, relatives of sea anemones and corals. They drift about on the surface of the ocean, using their weak muscles to move against the waves. Many become stranded on beaches. Jellyfish capture fishes and other prey with stinging cells located on tentacles that hang beneath the jellylike bell.

The **Moon Jelly** (46) is often seen in immense numbers along the eastern coast. It is mostly transparent, but has four rings in its center, which are actually its reproductive organs. In males these are pink and in females they are white. Tentacles are short.

The **Purple Jellyfish** (47) is a deepwater species that sometimes washes ashore. It has eight long, purplish tentacles and a maroon-red bell.

Sea Nettle (48) is a 4- to 7-inch jellyfish, found from Cape Cod south. Like the plant of the same name, Sea Nettle can give an irritating, painful sting. It is often found in bays and estuaries, and swimmers should avoid it. Mostly transparent, Sea Nettle has pale orange tentacles.

The largest jellyfish in our area is the **Lion's Mane** (49), which can reach a diameter of 8 feet! Most are considerably smaller. The northernmost populations are bright red; those to the south tend to be paler orange and yellow.

Hydroids

Also coelenterates, hydroids are colonial. What appears to be a single animal is actually a complex colony of individuals, each specialized for a certain task. Some hydroid colonies resemble tiny plants and are attached to rocks and shells. Others look superficially like jellyfish. Some have very powerful stinging cells.

Tubularians (50) are common hydroids, often found in the intertidal zone. The main feeding bodies, called polyps, have several rings of tentacles. The overall colony is usually pink. A close look at a tubularian colony will often reveal one or more nudibranchs, like the rusty brown **Striped Nudibranch (51)**, feeding on the polyps. Another hydroid dweller is the **Skeleton Shrimp (52)**. Not a true shrimp, this diminutive animal climbs about among the hydroids, seeking tiny prey.

Gonionemus (53) looks like a tiny jellyfish but is actually a hydroid. Less than an inch wide, it has up to 80 tentacles. Mostly translucent, it is strongly tinged with yellow.

The most infamous hydroid is **Physalia**, the **Portuguese Man-of-War (54)**. With a balloonlike float fully 12 inches long, and stinging tentacles that can extend 50 feet, this warm-water hydroid can pack a mighty wallop. Though dangerous, Physalia is beautiful, with shades of lavender and pink on the float and tentacles, and bright pinkish red along the upper margin of the float. Physalia often wash ashore and are to be avoided: even a beached Physalia can sting.

The **By-the-Wind Sailor (55)** is a small (4-inch) hydroid found in warm waters such as the Gulf Stream. The brownish float has a sail-like extension with a deep blue edge. The stinging tentacles are short.

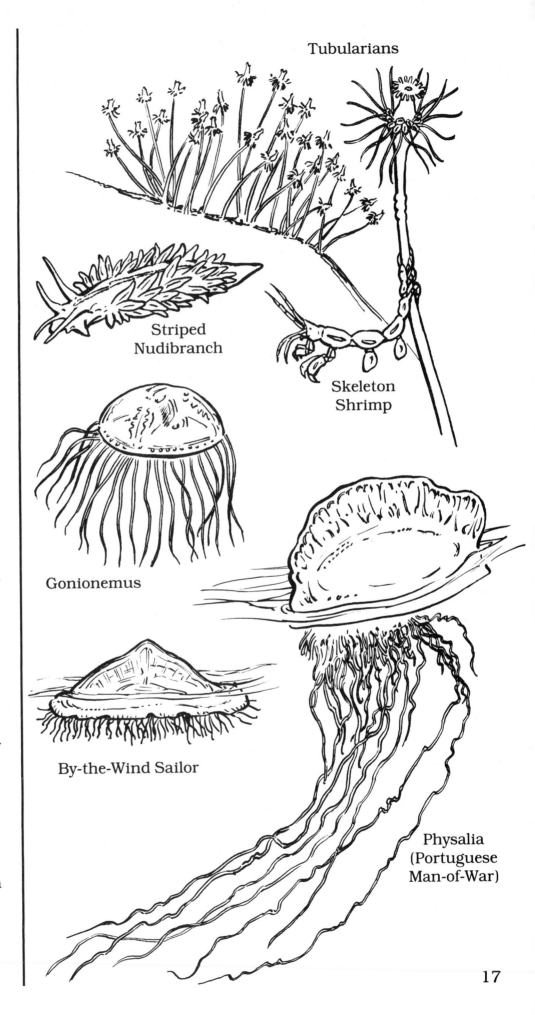

Tubularians

Striped
Nudibranch

Skeleton
Shrimp

Gonionemus

By-the-Wind Sailor

Physalia
(Portuguese
Man-of-War)

17

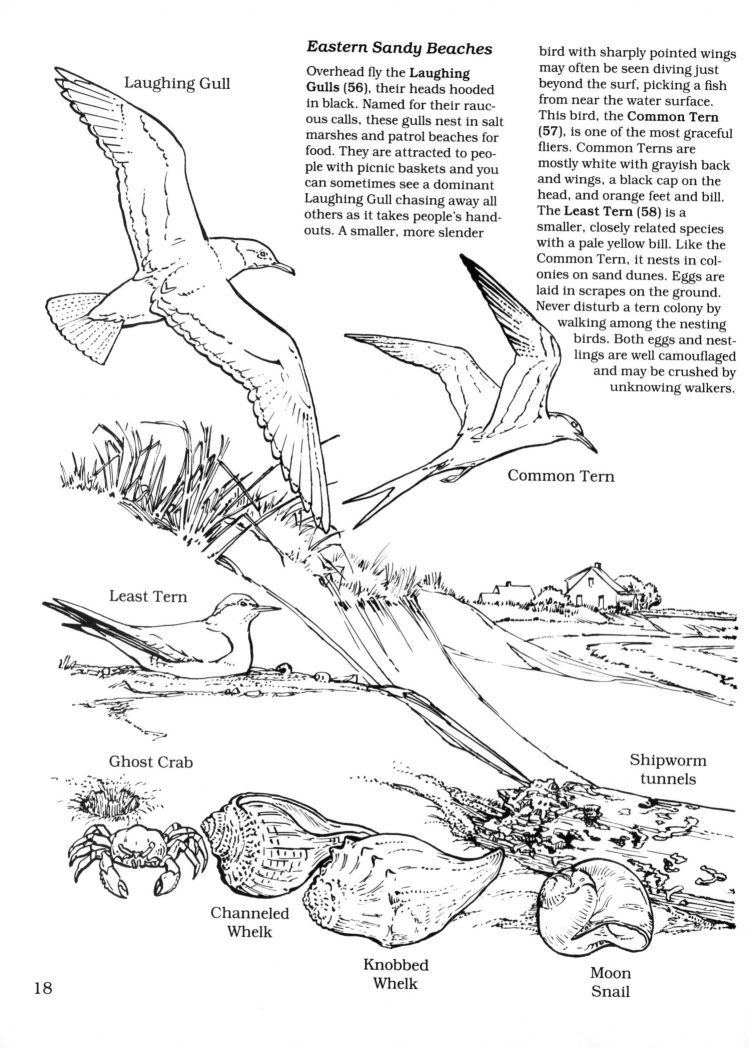

Laughing Gull

Eastern Sandy Beaches

Overhead fly the **Laughing Gulls (56)**, their heads hooded in black. Named for their raucous calls, these gulls nest in salt marshes and patrol beaches for food. They are attracted to people with picnic baskets and you can sometimes see a dominant Laughing Gull chasing away all others as it takes people's handouts. A smaller, more slender bird with sharply pointed wings may often be seen diving just beyond the surf, picking a fish from near the water surface. This bird, the **Common Tern (57)**, is one of the most graceful fliers. Common Terns are mostly white with grayish back and wings, a black cap on the head, and orange feet and bill. The **Least Tern (58)** is a smaller, closely related species with a pale yellow bill. Like the Common Tern, it nests in colonies on sand dunes. Eggs are laid in scrapes on the ground. Never disturb a tern colony by walking among the nesting birds. Both eggs and nestlings are well camouflaged and may be crushed by unknowing walkers.

Common Tern

Least Tern

Ghost Crab

Shipworm tunnels

Channeled Whelk

Knobbed Whelk

Moon Snail

18

Two smaller birds are often seen running on the beach, one near the waves, and the other on the upper beach. **Sanderling** flocks scurry at the waves' edge, picking up worms and other animals exposed by wave action. Sanderlings **(59)** are a species of sandpiper. They migrate from South America to nest in the Arctic. In spring they are rufous, their breeding plumage, but they turn gray as they return from their nesting grounds in midsummer. The **Piping Plover (60)** is so well camouflaged that many fail to notice the little bird until it gives its "piping" call. Pale gray above and white below, with a black slash on the neck, the plover seems to melt into the sand when it stops moving. Its bill and legs are bright yellow. Piping Plovers nest on the upper beach near sand dunes. Be careful not to disturb their nests.

Beachcombing will give you a look into the lives of some of the millions of marine animals. Large holes in the sand are the burrows of **Ghost Crabs (61)**. These pale crabs with black, stalked eyes scurry swiftly across the beach at night. A piece of driftwood is riddled with the tunnels of **Shipworms (62)**, which are long, slender clams with tiny shells. They burrow through wood, eating the wood as they go. In bygone eras, many wooden ships were sunk by leaks caused by Shipworms. You may see an odd collar of sand that was constructed on the beach by the **Atlantic Moon Snail (63)**, which lays hundreds of tiny eggs within the collar. If you see a **Surf Clam** shell **(64)**, look for a tiny hole the size of a BB near the apex of the shell. This hole was made by a Moon Snail, which drilled through the shell to eat the clam within. A string of dried, yellowish, coin-shaped objects is really the egg cases **(65)** of a **Channeled Whelk (66)** or the similar **Knobbed Whelk (67)**. Whelks, like Moon Snails, prey on clams and other invertebrates, but they break their prey's shell rather than drill through it. Inside the parchmentlike egg cases are many hundreds of tiny whelks. A baglike, dried black object **(68)** with four curved "horns" is called a "mermaid's purse." It is also an egg case, but not of a snail. Inside grows a tiny skate, a fish closely related to the sharks.

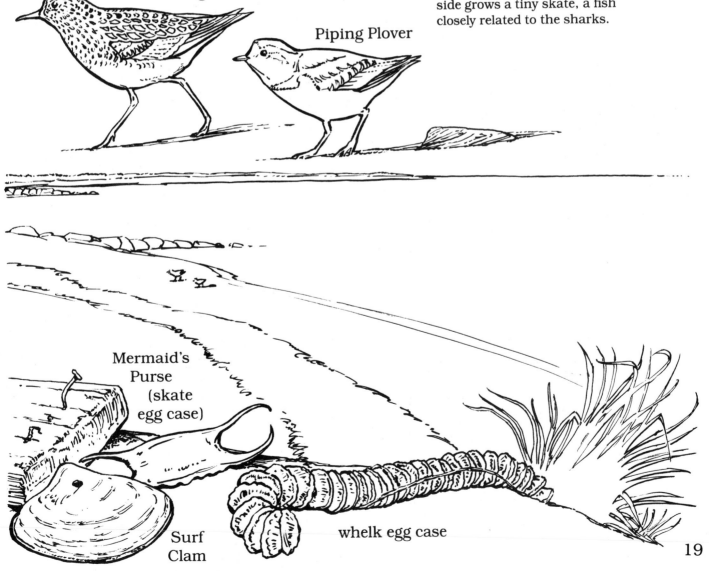

Sanderling

Piping Plover

Mermaid's
Purse
(skate
egg case)

Surf
Clam

whelk egg case

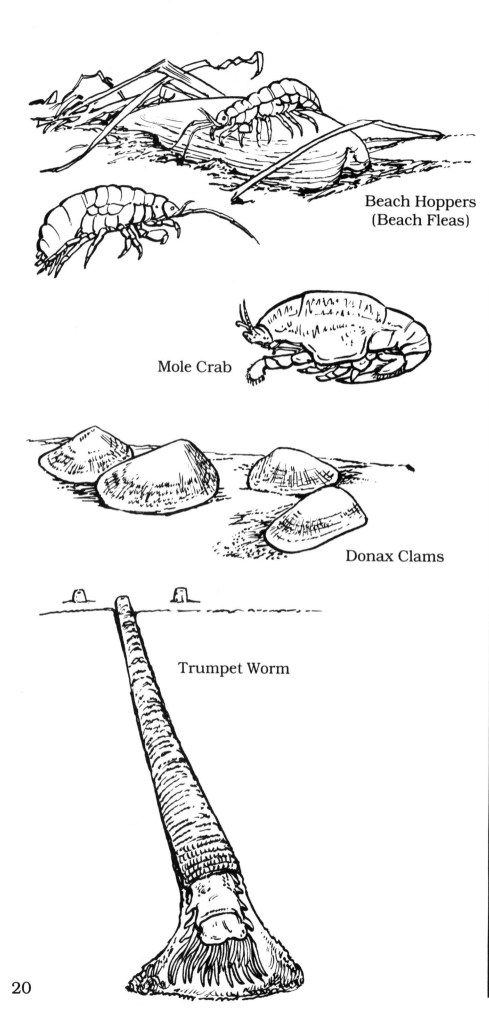

Beach Hoppers
(Beach Fleas)

Mole Crab

Donax Clams

Trumpet Worm

Small Sand-dwellers

Among the washed-up seaweed you will probably find dozens of tiny crustaceans called **beach hoppers** or **beach fleas** (69). They are not fleas, but they do hop. Several species, which look much alike, inhabit beach debris and burrow in the sand. They are members of a group called **amphipods**, or side-swimmers. Most are pale brown, the color of sand. They need moist sand to keep their gills wet. They generally avoid the sun and are active mostly at night.

A **mole crab** (70) is a grayish pink creature shaped a bit like a football. Mole crabs move up and down the beach with the waves. As a wave retreats, many mole crabs emerge from the sand, scurry along with the wave, and quickly reburrow. Their streamlined body shape is an aid in rapid burrowing. Their feathery antennae are used to capture tiny food particles. They neither pinch nor bite.

Large colonies of **donax clams** (71) live along the shore, in or near the area washed by waves. Thousands may have burrowed just beneath the surface of the sand. Hundreds of these clams may be suddenly exposed beneath your feet by the rushing surf. Watch them as they burrow, disappearing beneath the sand with surprising quickness. These tiny, wedge-shaped clams come in many colors. Northern species are yellowish, with faint purple rays. The **Coquina**, a donax clam found in Florida, is pale with rays of bright orange, pink, or even blue.

The 2-inch **Trumpet Worm** (72) is the master builder of the beach. This creature, which has a brilliant gold head and tentacles, constructs a carefully crafted, cone-shaped tube of sand grains it has cemented together. The worm resides inside its tube, feeding on tiny food particles that are washed along.

20

Beyond the Waves

The **Lady Crab (73)** is common in waters with sandy bottoms. Its shed shell, or carapace, is often washed ashore. It is a swimming crab, and its last pair of legs are flattened into paddles. The carapace is mottled reddish brown, the claws are orange, and the swimming legs are yellow. Like most crabs, the Lady Crab scavenges for food.

The **Blue Crab (74)** is one of our most important shellfish. This crab of the Chesapeake Bay region is a popular delicacy. Like the Lady Crab, it too is a swimming crab. Its powerful claws can give a sharp pinch. The carapace is olive, but the legs and claws are bright blue fringed with orange. Blue Crabs live offshore and in estuaries.

The 10-inch **Mantis Shrimp (75)** is not commonly seen, as it burrows in sand below the tide line and is active mostly at night. Named for their vague resemblance to a praying mantis, Mantis Shrimp, like their insect namesakes, are voracious predators of shrimps, fishes, and anything else they can catch in their formidable front appendages. The body is pinkish brown outlined in green and yellow, and the eyes are brilliant green.

In its own way as odd as the Mantis Shrimp, the **Sea Mouse (76)** is a wide-bodied, 6- to 9-inch worm, covered with a colorful furry coat and tiny bristles. The "fur" glistens with iridescent greens, browns, and golds. This worm lives offshore, combing the bottom for food, but is sometimes washed ashore after a severe storm. The Sea Mouse's scientific name, *Aphrodita*, comes from the Greek goddess Aphrodite — an odd choice for a fat worm.

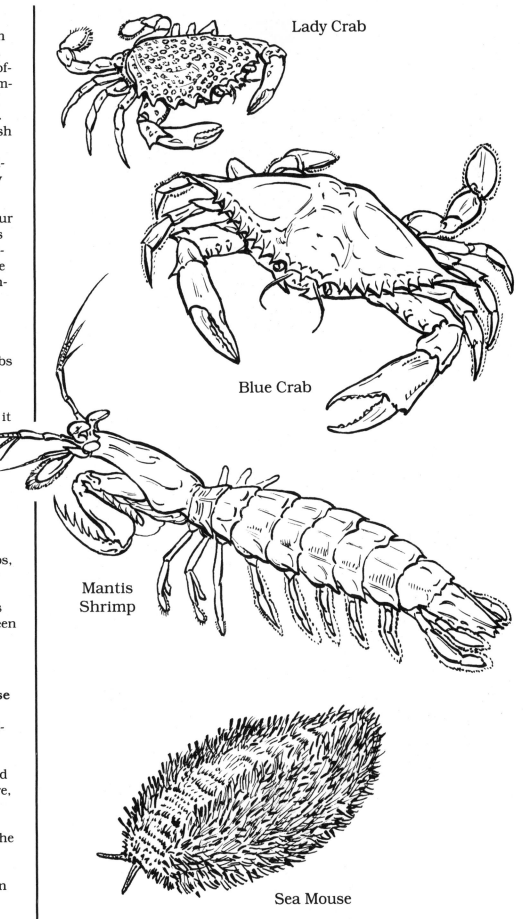

Lady Crab

Blue Crab

Mantis Shrimp

Sea Mouse

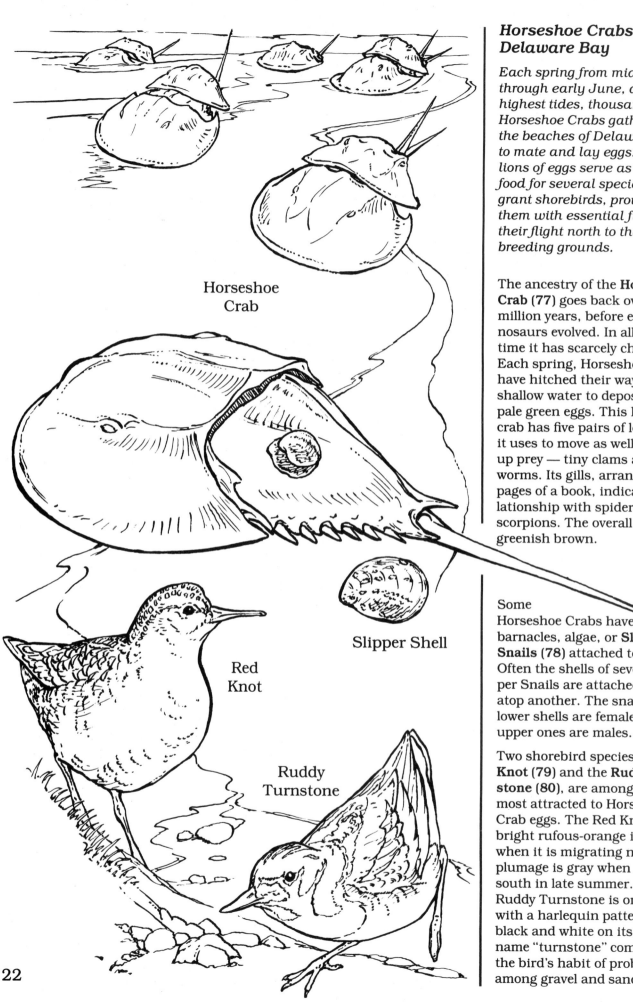

Horseshoe
Crab

Slipper Shell

Red
Knot

Ruddy
Turnstone

Horseshoe Crabs and Delaware Bay

Each spring from mid-May through early June, during the highest tides, thousands of Horseshoe Crabs gather along the beaches of Delaware Bay to mate and lay eggs. The billions of eggs serve as a key food for several species of migrant shorebirds, providing them with essential fuel for their flight north to their arctic breeding grounds.

The ancestry of the **Horseshoe Crab (77)** goes back over 300 million years, before even the dinosaurs evolved. In all of that time it has scarcely changed. Each spring, Horseshoe Crabs have hitched their way into shallow water to deposit their pale green eggs. This harmless crab has five pairs of legs, which it uses to move as well as to pick up prey — tiny clams and worms. Its gills, arranged like pages of a book, indicate its relationship with spiders and scorpions. The overall color is greenish brown.

Some Horseshoe Crabs have barnacles, algae, or **Slipper Snails (78)** attached to them. Often the shells of several Slipper Snails are attached, one atop another. The snails in the lower shells are females, and the upper ones are males.

Two shorebird species, the **Red Knot (79)** and the **Ruddy Turnstone (80)**, are among the birds most attracted to Horseshoe Crab eggs. The Red Knot is bright rufous-orange in spring when it is migrating north. Its plumage is gray when it flies south in late summer. The Ruddy Turnstone is orange-red with a harlequin pattern of black and white on its face. The name "turnstone" comes from the bird's habit of probing among gravel and sand for food.

Swift Swimmers of the Open Sea

The **Striped Bass** (81) is one of the most popular game fishes. It is often caught by surfcasting with a rod and reel. A fully grown adult can reach a length of 5 feet. These fish are dark olive-green above and white below, with black spotting in rows along the sides. Striped Bass, also known as "Rockfish," spawn in estuaries and rivers; their numbers have been reduced by pollution.

Bluefish (82) are popular table treats. They appear in Florida by midwinter and move northward, satisfying seafood lovers all the way to New England. Bluefish schools are the "wolf packs" of the ocean: they attack schools of smaller fish with their powerful jaws and sharp teeth. Adults can reach a length

Striped Bass

of 3 feet. Bluefish are shiny blue-green above and silver-white below.

The streamlined **Atlantic Bonito** (83) is also a popular table fish, often caught on rod and reel. The Bonito is steel blue above and yellowish on the sides, with shades of pink below. Black striping lines its upper sides.

Schools of **Long-finned Squid** (84) are often preyed upon by Bluefish and tunas. Squids are mollusks, closely related to octopuses, but much more streamlined and swift. They can swim equally well forwards or backwards. Squids capture food using 10 tentacles armed with suction cups. Long-finned Squid are translucent reddish, with black and orange spotting.

Long-finned Squid

Bluefish

Atlantic Bonito

23

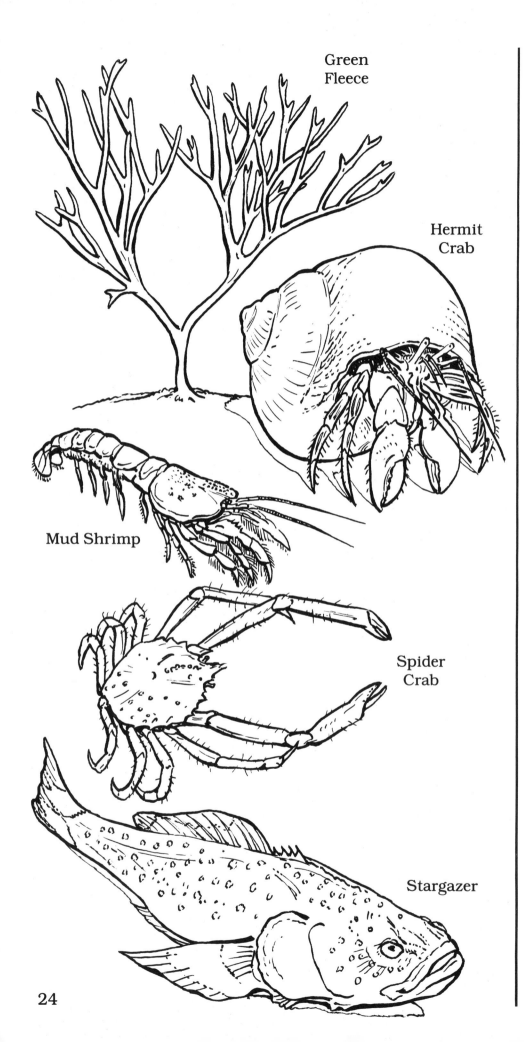

Green
Fleece

Hermit
Crab

Mud Shrimp

Spider
Crab

Stargazer

Mudflats

Around salt marshes, bays, and estuaries, when the tide is low, vast expanses of mudflats are often revealed. If you are armed with a shovel and pail, and are willing to get your feet wet and a bit muddy, you will find that these flats contain an abundance of burrowing creatures that are fed upon by various fishes and birds.

Green Fleece (85) is a green alga, or seaweed, that was accidentally introduced from Europe to the mid-Atlantic seashore. It grows in estuaries and is commonly washed up on flats. This bright green plant can grow so densely that it chokes shellfish beds.

Hermit crabs (86) are common sights as they amble about mudflats in search of food tidbits or a larger empty shell to move into. Most species are pinkish with orange legs.

Mud shrimps (87) of several species build communal burrows in the mud. These pale gray creatures rarely leave the protection of their burrows. They feed on tiny animals washed in with the tides.

Spider crabs (88) look menacing but are quite harmless: their claws can barely pinch. The carapace (shell) of these yellowish brown crabs is only 4 inches long, but the arms are relatively long, giving the animal a span of 12 inches. Spider crabs feed on whatever edible material they can find.

With its eyes located on the top of its head, the **Stargazer (89)** is always looking upward. This 12-inch fish, rich brown with white speckling, buries itself in muddy sand. Be careful not to handle this fish. Just behind its eyes are specialized muscles capable of giving off an electric shock! The shock may help it procure small fishes and crustaceans for food, as well as protect it.

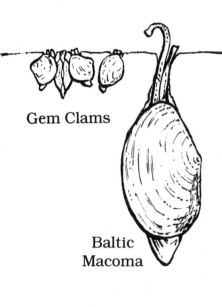

Gem Clams

Baltic
Macoma

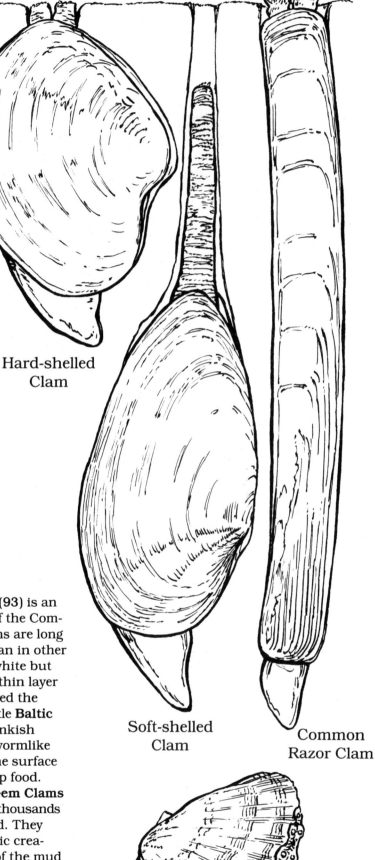

Stout
Tagelus

Hard-shelled
Clam

Soft-shelled
Clam

Common
Razor Clam

Bay
Scallop

Shellfish of the Flats

Some of our tastiest seafood morsels come from mudflats. Other species, less tempting to the palate, share the mud. All clams are filter feeders. They take in water through one siphon tube, filter it for food and oxygen, and expel it through another siphon tube.

The **Soft-shelled Clam (90)** (also known as the "Steamer" and "Gaper") burrows deeply, extending its long grayish pink siphons to the surface of its burrow. As you walk across a mudflat, you might get squirted as the clams detect your vibrations in the mud. Like most burrowing clams, soft-shells use their pinkish, wedge-shaped muscular foot to dig. As the name implies, the white shell breaks easily. Another palate pleaser is the **Hard-shelled Clam (91)**, or **Quahog**. This species, which tends to be found in less muddy areas than soft-shells, makes shallow burrows because its siphon tubes are short. Small hard-shells are called "cherrystones." The **Common Razor Clam (92)** is easily identified by its elongate bluish shell, like an old-fashioned razor case. Razor clams burrow quite deeply and can easily escape the would-be clammer.

The **Stout Tagelus (93)** is an abbreviated version of the Common Razor. Its siphons are long and more separate than in other species. The shell is white but is partly covered by a thin layer of brown material called the periostracum. The little **Baltic Macoma (94)** has a pinkish white shell and long wormlike siphons that sweep the surface of the mud, picking up food. Tiny purplish white **Gem Clams (95)** may occur by the thousands buried in shallow mud. They too feed on microscopic creatures. At the surface of the mud the **Bay Scallop (96)**, snaps its shell shut, forcing out water that sends it randomly spinning away in the water.

25

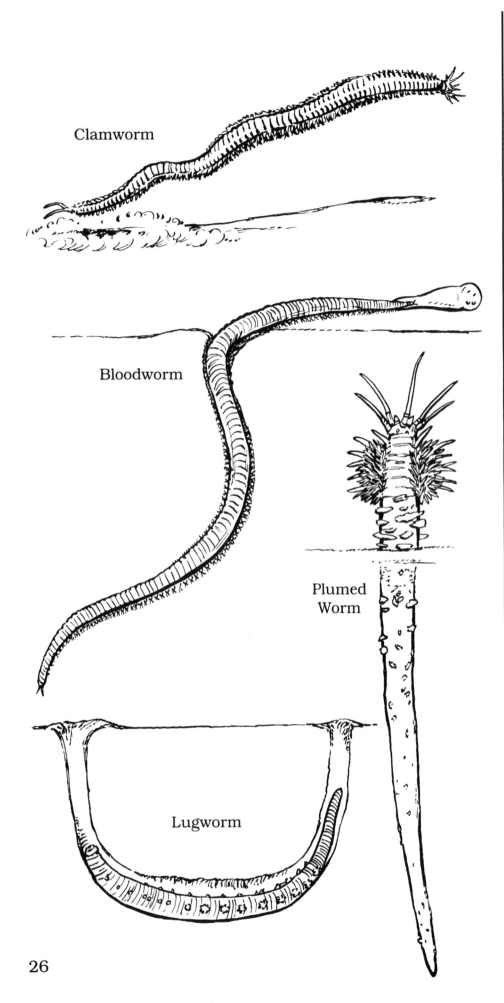

Clamworm

Bloodworm

Plumed
Worm

Lugworm

Segmented Worms

Mudflats are riddled with worm burrows. Most marine worm species are segmented. Many species live in tubes, feeding on food that washes in or is procured on the surface. Other worms emerge and swim freely in search of prey. The diversity of marine worms will amaze you.

The **Clamworm (97)** is dull green with tinges of yellow. This common worm can reach a length of 8 inches. It swims well, using fleshy paddles on each body segment. The mouth parts, containing sharp jaws, are normally contracted (like the head of a turtle in its shell) but can be everted (turned inside out) to catch prey.

The **Bloodworm (98)** is well named. Commonly used to bait fish hooks, this rusty green worm has red blood. Bloodworms have a very long, muscular proboscis armed with four small hooks that they can shoot forward to capture prey. The hooks can nip a finger, so be careful handling these worms.

The **Plumed Worm (99)** builds a tube that projects a few inches above the mud surface and can extend to 3 feet deep! The tube is made of leathery material embedded with tiny bits of shell. The worm itself is iridescent greenish with bright red gill tufts.

The **Lugworm (100)** builds a U-shaped burrow that is open at both ends. Look for the two holes. The 8-inch worm inside is olive-green with tufts of small yellow bristles and red gill tufts. Lugworms are thickest toward the front. They ingest mud and remove organic matter from it in much the same way as earthworms do in soil.

The **Terebellid Worm (101)** has a dense tuft of soft tentacles on its head. The worm builds a short mud tube in a burrow, and collects organic matter by sweeping the mud surface with its tentacles. The worm's body is grayish yellow, the tentacles are tan, and there is a tuft of red gills near the mouth.

Fringed Worms (102) also have long tentacles, which they use to sweep the surface for food. Their long pinkish tentacles and red gills are delicate and easily broken.

Fanworms (103) live in leathery tubes covered with mud and sand. Only their heads protrude, showing two large fanlike tufts that sweep the water for food particles. Fanworms do not burrow. They attach their tubes to rocks, shells, and other solid objects.

Bamboo Worms (104) are named for their segment arrangement that resembles the stem of a bamboo plant. The color is usually grayish white with red where the segments join. These long, thin, easily damaged worms live in tubes in the mud.

The **Parchment Worm (105)** has perhaps the most unusual body structure of any segmented worm. Its overall color is brownish yellow. The worm inhabits a parchmentlike, U-shaped tube that protrudes above the mud on both ends. The worm uses its flimsy body paddles to move water through the tube, removing food and oxygen from the water.

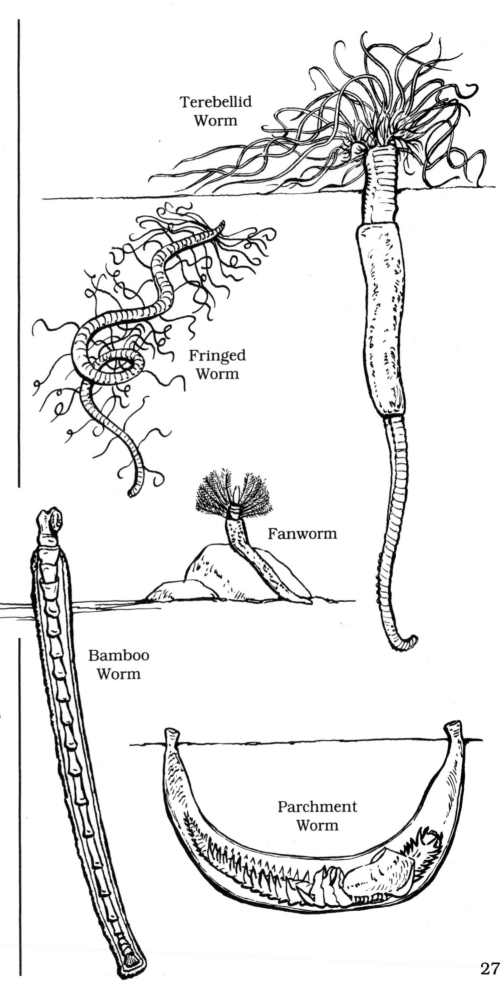

Terebellid Worm

Fringed Worm

Fanworm

Bamboo Worm

Parchment Worm

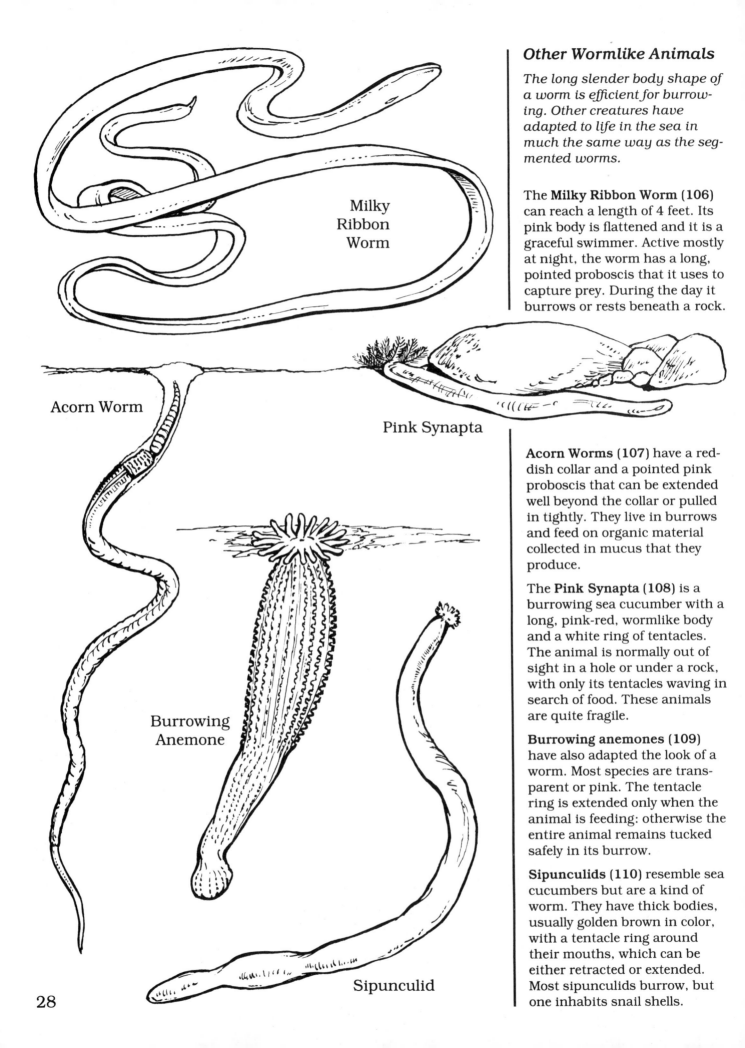

Milky
Ribbon
Worm

Acorn Worm

Pink Synapta

Burrowing
Anemone

Sipunculid

Other Wormlike Animals

The long slender body shape of a worm is efficient for burrowing. Other creatures have adapted to life in the sea in much the same way as the segmented worms.

The **Milky Ribbon Worm (106)** can reach a length of 4 feet. Its pink body is flattened and it is a graceful swimmer. Active mostly at night, the worm has a long, pointed proboscis that it uses to capture prey. During the day it burrows or rests beneath a rock.

Acorn Worms (107) have a reddish collar and a pointed pink proboscis that can be extended well beyond the collar or pulled in tightly. They live in burrows and feed on organic material collected in mucus that they produce.

The **Pink Synapta (108)** is a burrowing sea cucumber with a long, pink-red, wormlike body and a white ring of tentacles. The animal is normally out of sight in a hole or under a rock, with only its tentacles waving in search of food. These animals are quite fragile.

Burrowing anemones (109) have also adapted the look of a worm. Most species are transparent or pink. The tentacle ring is extended only when the animal is feeding; otherwise the entire animal remains tucked safely in its burrow.

Sipunculids (110) resemble sea cucumbers but are a kind of worm. They have thick bodies, usually golden brown in color, with a tentacle ring around their mouths, which can be either retracted or extended. Most sipunculids burrow, but one inhabits snail shells.

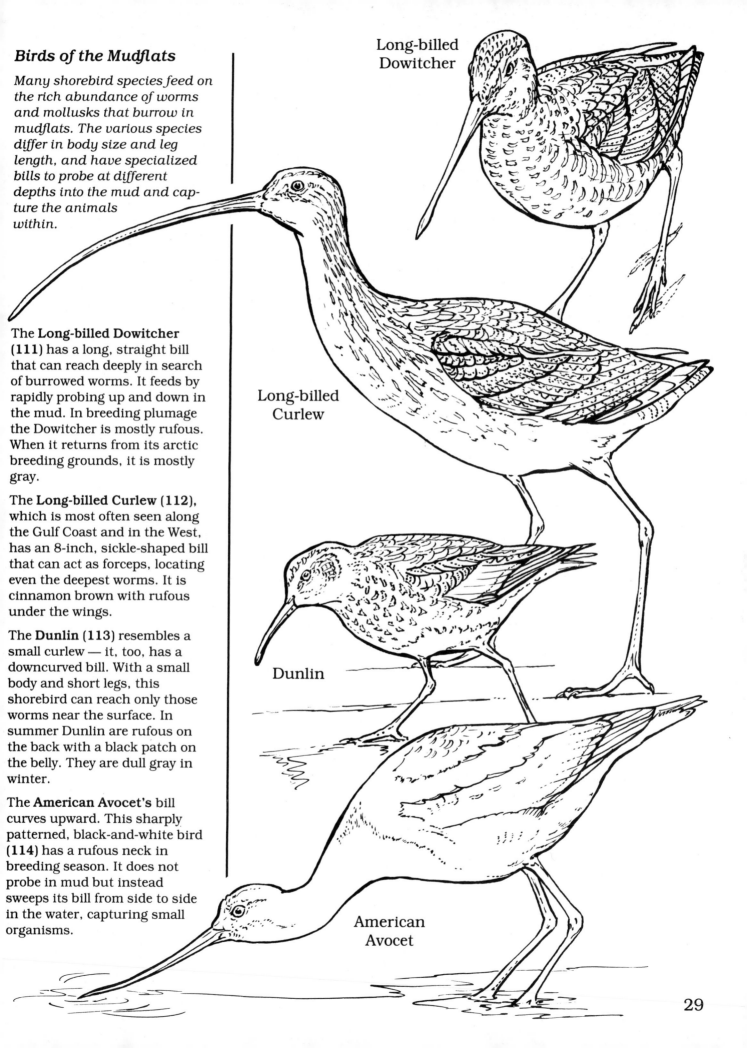

Birds of the Mudflats

Many shorebird species feed on the rich abundance of worms and mollusks that burrow in mudflats. The various species differ in body size and leg length, and have specialized bills to probe at different depths into the mud and capture the animals within.

The **Long-billed Dowitcher** **(111)** has a long, straight bill that can reach deeply in search of burrowed worms. It feeds by rapidly probing up and down in the mud. In breeding plumage the Dowitcher is mostly rufous. When it returns from its arctic breeding grounds, it is mostly gray.

The **Long-billed Curlew (112)**, which is most often seen along the Gulf Coast and in the West, has an 8-inch, sickle-shaped bill that can act as forceps, locating even the deepest worms. It is cinnamon brown with rufous under the wings.

The **Dunlin (113)** resembles a small curlew — it, too, has a downcurved bill. With a small body and short legs, this shorebird can reach only those worms near the surface. In summer Dunlin are rufous on the back with a black patch on the belly. They are dull gray in winter.

The **American Avocet's** bill curves upward. This sharply patterned, black-and-white bird **(114)** has a rufous neck in breeding season. It does not probe in mud but instead sweeps its bill from side to side in the water, capturing small organisms.

Long-billed
Dowitcher

Long-billed
Curlew

Dunlin

American
Avocet

29

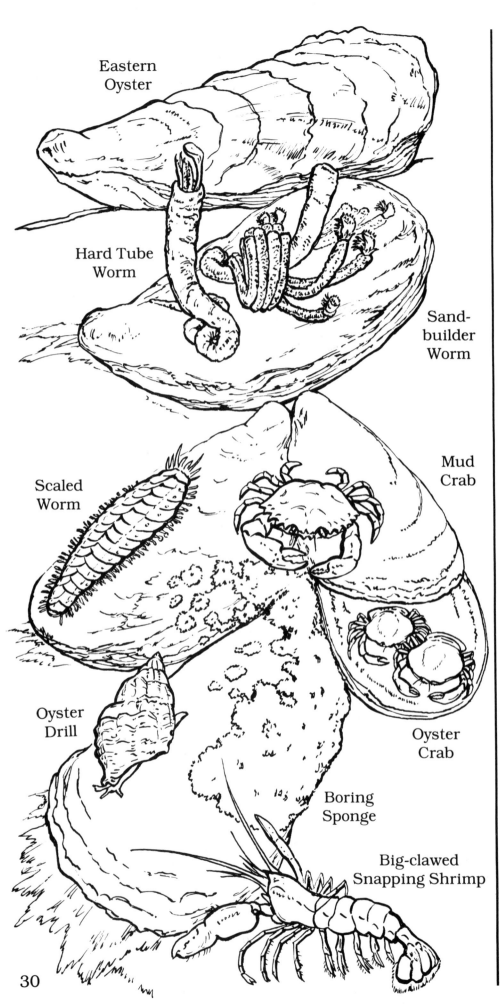

Eastern
Oyster

Hard Tube
Worm

Sand-
builder
Worm

Mud
Crab

Scaled
Worm

Oyster
Drill

Oyster
Crab

Boring
Sponge

Big-clawed
Snapping Shrimp

Oyster Bars

Oysters form dense aggregations called "bars." An ecological community of many species lives among the oysters. Oyster bars are not intertidal: they are found at depths ranging from 8 to 25 feet.

The **Eastern Oyster** (115) feeds on tiny plankton, which are filtered from the water when the oyster opens its paired shells. Like barnacles, oyster larvae settle permanently, never moving from their chosen site. Because oysters do not burrow or swim, many other animals settle on them.

Sand-builder Worms (116) often build their curved brownish tubes of cemented sand grains on oyster shells. The worm pokes its head, covered by bright golden bristles, outside the tube when it feeds.

Several species of **hard tube worms** (117) build their little white tubes on oyster shells.

Scaled worms do not build tubes. They are flattened and can cling tightly to any surface. This species (118) is purplish red, with yellow bristles.

Mud crabs (119) live among the oysters. Most are less than an inch long and are brown with black tips on their claws.

The tiny **Oyster Crab** (120), barely ½ inch long, lives within the oyster itself and takes some of the oyster's food.

The **Oyster Drill** (121) is a small snail that preys on oysters. It drills through the shell and devours the oyster inside.

The yellow **Boring Sponge** (122) bores into and can overgrow an oyster shell, killing the animal within.

The greenish gray **Big-clawed Snapping Shrimp** (123) is named for the popping sound made by the large claw.

Eelgrass Flat

Eelgrass (124) is not an alga but is a marine plant related to freshwater pondweeds. Its long green blades grow in shallow protected areas near salt marshes. Many animal species live among the underwater meadows of Eelgrass.

Three kinds of fish are quite partial to Eelgrass. **Pipefishes** and **seahorses** are closely related and live similar kinds of lives. Males brood the babies in a unique pouch on the male's abdomen. **Pipefishes (125)** are brownish green with yellow on the belly, but can change color to blend with their backgrounds. **Seahorses (126)** are light yellow-brown. Both fishes are speckled with white dots and dark mottlings, and both can be hard to find as they are well camouflaged in the Eelgrass. **Sticklebacks (127)** are named for the sharp spines near the uppermost fin. Several species occur. Most are variable in color, usually greenish brown above and silvery on the sides. However, during breeding season these fish become quite reddish, especially below. The males guard nests made of vegetation stuck together with mucus.

The little **Eelgrass Slug (128)** is a light yellow-green nudibranch (sea slug). It is common to Eelgrass meadows but is hard to find, as it is so well camouflaged. Scoop up some Eelgrass in a net and look closely for it.

You may also find the brown **Eelgrass Pillbug (129)** among the blades. Pillbugs are crustaceans called isopods. Another species, the **Elongated Eelgrass Isopod (130)**, is easy to recognize by its wormlike shape.

At the base of the Eelgrass stalks are the tubes of **tube-making amphipods**. Several species, such as the **Slender Tube-maker (131)** shown here, build tubes of mud, sand, and debris. Some live in dense colonies.

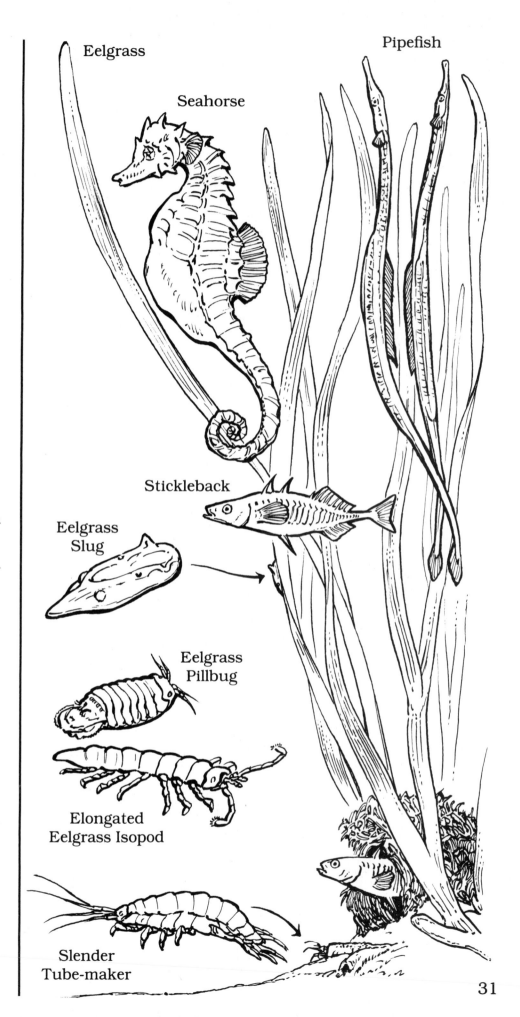

Eelgrass

Pipefish

Seahorse

Stickleback

Eelgrass Slug

Eelgrass Pillbug

Elongated Eelgrass Isopod

Slender Tube-maker

31

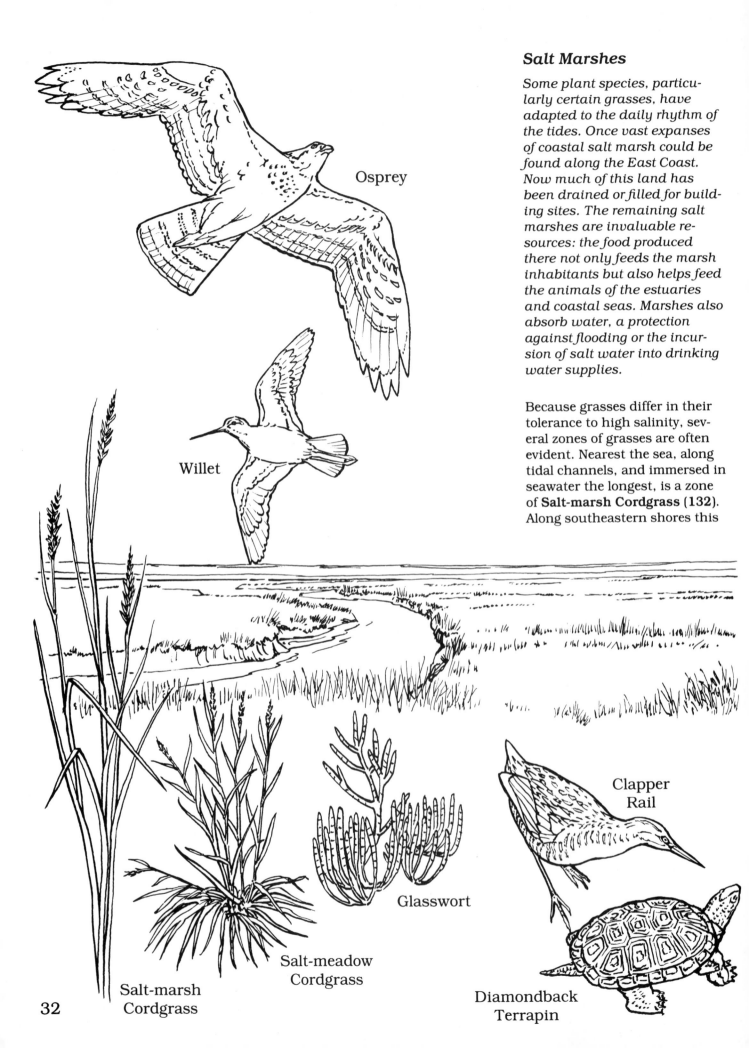

Osprey

Salt Marshes

Some plant species, particularly certain grasses, have adapted to the daily rhythm of the tides. Once vast expanses of coastal salt marsh could be found along the East Coast. Now much of this land has been drained or filled for building sites. The remaining salt marshes are invaluable resources: the food produced there not only feeds the marsh inhabitants but also helps feed the animals of the estuaries and coastal seas. Marshes also absorb water, a protection against flooding or the incursion of salt water into drinking water supplies.

Because grasses differ in their tolerance to high salinity, several zones of grasses are often evident. Nearest the sea, along tidal channels, and immersed in seawater the longest, is a zone of **Salt-marsh Cordgrass (132)**. Along southeastern shores this

Willet

Clapper Rail

Glasswort

Salt-meadow Cordgrass

Salt-marsh Cordgrass

Diamondback Terrapin

grass can top 8 feet. Behind this zone grows **Salt-meadow Cordgrass (133)**, a shorter, thinner grass that grows as a tousled mat resembling "cowlicks." Several species of **glasswort (134)** grow among the cordgrasses, often forming dense mats. Glassworts become bright orange-red in fall. Higher in the marsh you'll find **Salt Reed (135)**, a tall yellowish brown grass with large brown seed tufts.

Salt marshes abound with birds. Overhead you may hear the sharp whistles of the **Osprey (136)**. This majestic, blackish brown and white bird plunges into the water feet first to capture fish. The shaggy crested **Belted Kingfisher (137)** dives headfirst for fish. Males and females are grayish blue above and white below, but only the females have the rufous belly band. The **Willet (138)** is a large grayish sandpiper with bold, black-and-white patterning under its wings. Willets nest on the ground in salt marshes. Skulking among the marsh grasses and searching for food along the tidal channels, the **Clapper Rail (139)** is not nearly so obvious as a Willet. This grayish brown, chicken-sized bird is yellowish on its neck and has black barring along its flanks. Salt-marsh tidepools provide fishes for the all-white **Great Egret (140)** and the slate blue **Little Blue Heron (141)**. At night these same pools are visited by hungry **Black-crowned Night-Herons (142)**. These chunky waders have gray wings, a black back and head, and bright red eyes. The **Diamondback Terrapin (143)** is easily recognized by the diamondlike patterning on its gray shell. The head is light gray with black spotting.

Belted Kingfisher

Salt Reed

Great Egret

Little Blue Heron

Black-crowned Night-Heron

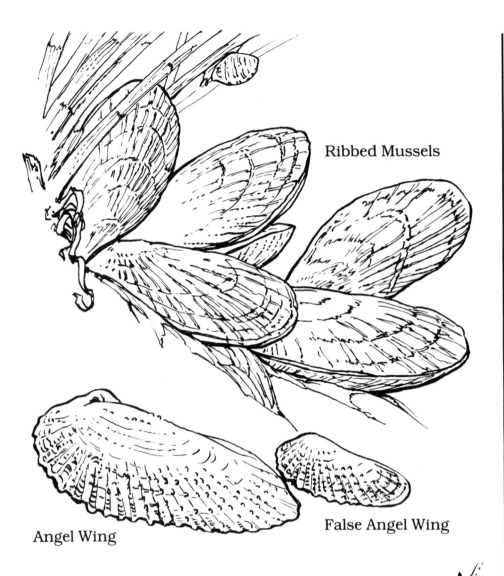

Ribbed Mussels

Angel Wing

False Angel Wing

Small Creatures of the Salt Marsh

Among the stems of the cordgrass are colonies of **Ribbed Mussels (144)**. These yellowish brown bivalves (paired shells) are named for the ridges that run along the shells. By constantly filtering water, mussels help concentrate nutrients, enhancing the fertility of the marsh.

Also burrowed among the mud and organic material (called peat) are two more bivalves, the **Angel Wing (145)** and **False Angel Wing (146)**. They are both white and look similar, though the Angel Wing is larger. The shells are shaped like sharpened wedges, an aid in burrowing through thick peat. Shells are generally fragile and broken pieces are common on beaches.

Grazing on the stalks of the cordgrasses, the little **Salt-marsh Snail (147)** is light brown with dark brown banding.

Grass Shrimp (148) are often abundant in tidal channels. These small creatures are nearly transparent, but they are often easy to observe as they congregate around a dead fish or other food source.

Also attracted to decaying material is the abundant **Mud Snail (149)**.

Grass Shrimp

Salt-marsh Snail

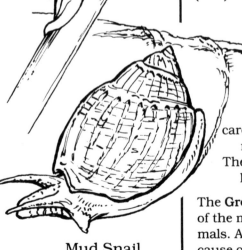

Mud Snail

Large numbers converge on carcasses and their trails are readily visible in the mud. These snails are dark brown, like the mud they inhabit.

The **Greenhead Fly (150)** is one of the most obvious marsh animals. A nuisance to people because of its painful bite, this large, bluish black fly has huge green compound eyes.

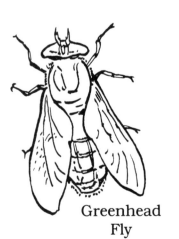

Greenhead Fly

Salt-marsh Fishes

Mummichogs, also known as **killifishes**, are abundant in salt-marsh channels and pools. Often called "minnows," they are frequently used as bait fish. They are small in body size but ecologically valuable, as they feed heavily on mosquito larvae. The **Mummichog (151)** is a husky fish and, at 6 inches long, is the largest killifish. Males in breeding condition are bluish black above, with a bright yellow belly. Females are olive, with paler fins. **Striped Killifish (152)** males have vertical black striping; females have horizontal stripes. In breeding condition males have bright orange bellies. Both sexes are greenish to black above, yellowish below.

Silversides (153) are slender, 3-inch fish with bright silvery bodies. They often occur in schools with killifish, feeding on tiny shrimps, worms, larvae, and fish eggs.

Shad (154) are also silvery fish, but they can reach lengths in excess of 2 feet. In spring, they migrate through salt marshes to fresh water in order to spawn. They spend the winter months in the ocean.

The **American Eel (155)** also migrates from the ocean to fresh water, but not to breed. All eels breed in the tropical Sargasso Sea in the South Atlantic Ocean. The young eels, called **glass eels** or **elvers**, migrate upstream by night, burrowing beneath stones during the day. They remain in estuaries and rivers until they are mature. At that time they return to the Sargasso Sea to breed. The adult eels are yellowish green.

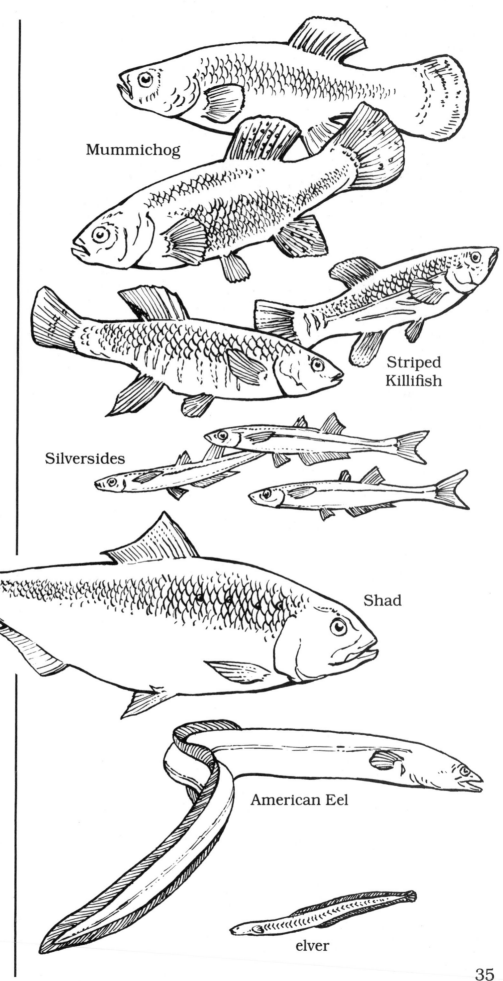

Mummichog

Striped
Killifish

Silversides

Shad

American Eel

elver

Sea Lavender

Salt-marsh
Fleabane

Seaside
Gerardia

Salt-marsh
Aster

Blue-eyed
Grass

Groundsel-
tree

Marsh
Elder

Salt-marsh Plants

Grasses and glassworts are not the only salt-marsh plants. Here are other colorful species to look for.

Sea Lavender (156), also called **Marsh Rosemary**, has large leaves that hug the ground. The many-branched stalk is lined with delicate light purple flowers in summer.

In late summer **Salt-marsh Fleabane (157)** blossoms along with **Salt-marsh Aster (158)**. Both are daisy-like, but the fleabane has dense pink-purple blossoms and the aster is white or light purple.

Seaside Gerardia (159) is a slender-leaved plant with rosy-purple, trumpetlike flowers that bloom from midsummer through early autumn.

Marsh Elder (160) is a shrubby plant about 3 feet tall, with small, yellow-white flowers and leaves in opposite pairs.

Groundsel-tree (161) is a shrub with two kinds of flowers that look different and are on separate trees. Male flowers have white "bristles," which the yellowish white female flowers lack.

Blue-eyed Grass (162) is not a grass at all but is a member of the lily family. The leaf blades resemble those of a grass, but the flower, blue-violet with a yellow center, reveals the plant's true identity.

36

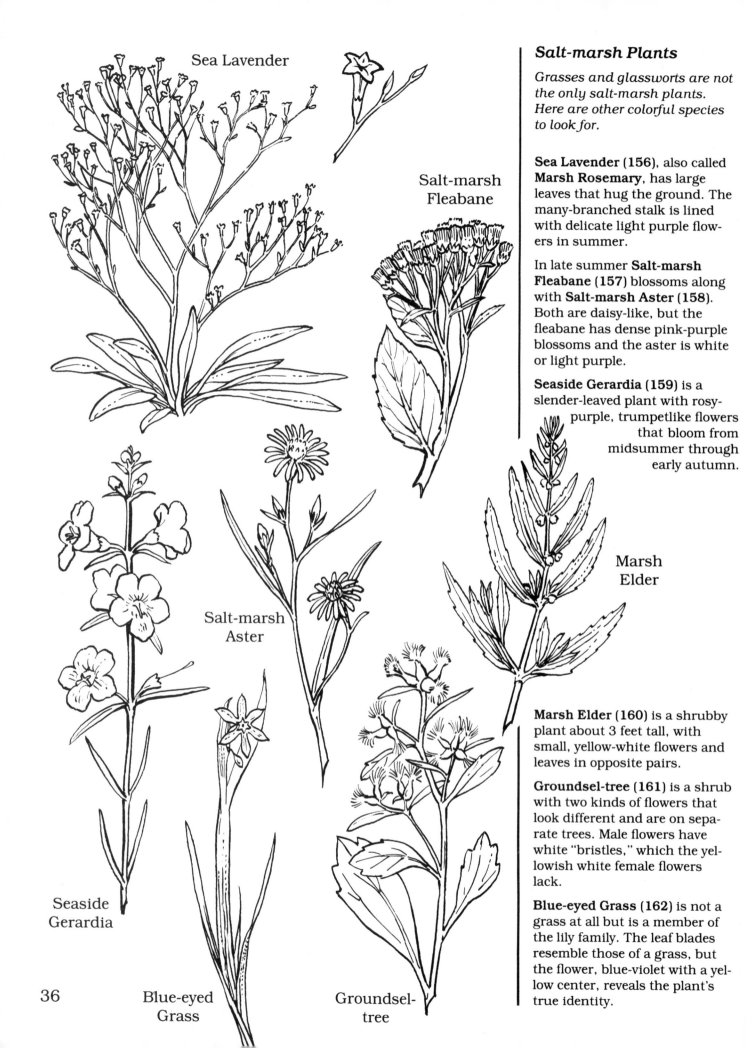

Land Birds of the Salt Marsh

Red-winged Blackbirds (163) are among the most obvious marsh birds. Males are glossy black with red wing epaulettes lined with yellow. They perch atop the grasses and sing *ee-oh-lay.* Females are smaller with brown streaks and resemble a large sparrow.

Tree Swallows (164) skim the marsh in pursuit of mosquitoes and other insect prey. Both sexes look the same: iridescent greenish blue above, bright white below.

Marsh Wrens (165) sing their gurgling songs from cordgrass stalks. Wrens are quite small. Both sexes are rufous brown with a white eyestripe and white streaking on the back.

Two sparrows, the **Sharp-tailed Sparrow (166)** and the **Seaside Sparrow (167)**, make their nests among the salt-marsh grasses. They skulk around and are best seen when they are singing atop a grass stalk. Sharp-tails have yellowish orange eyestripes. Seasides are darker brown, with only a small patch of yellow in front of the eye.

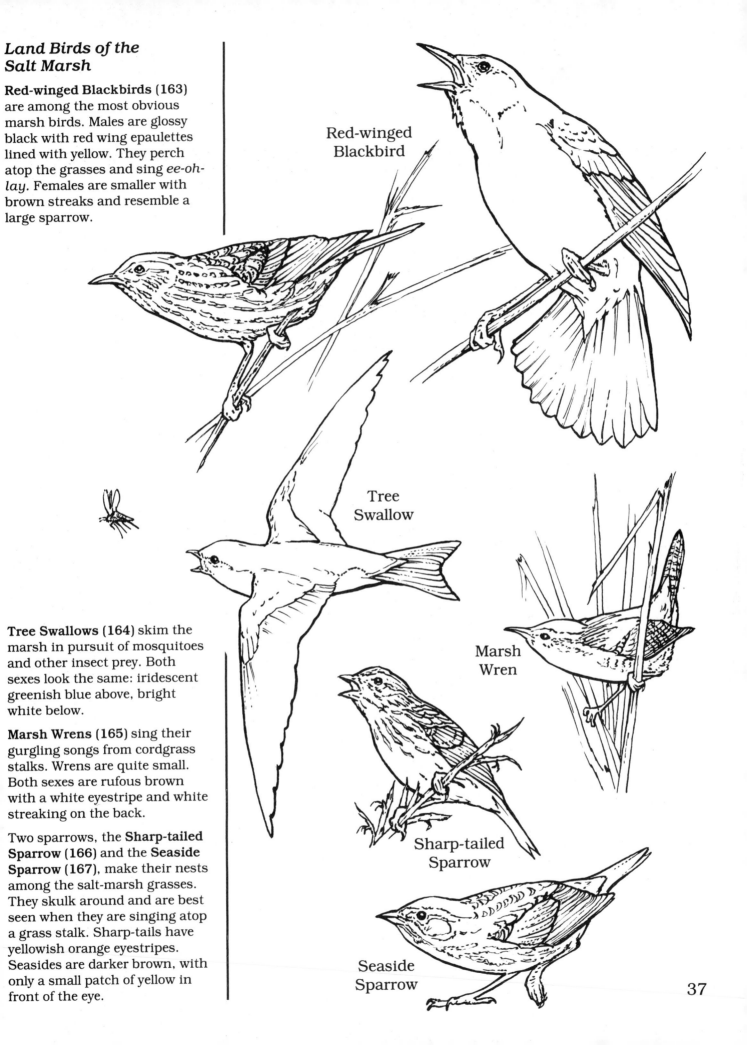

Red-winged
Blackbird

Tree
Swallow

Marsh
Wren

Sharp-tailed
Sparrow

Seaside
Sparrow

37

Black
Skimmer

Brown
Pelican

Red-breasted
Merganser

Surf
Scoter

American
Oyster-
catcher

Life in the Estuary

An estuary or bay is the place where fresh water from inland rivers meets salt water from the ocean. The daily cycle of tides mixes the water well. Estuaries are generally sheltered somewhat by barrier beaches or other features of coastal geography. Large numbers of fishes and other marine animals enter estuaries to breed. Sheltered in estuaries, young fishes and other animals thrive on the rich mixture of food washed into the bay by the river and tides. Many birds are also attracted to the estuary and its surrounding marshes as a place to feed and nest.

The **Black Skimmer (168)** is a sharply patterned black and white bird, often seen feeding in estuaries. The lower half of its black and red bill is much longer than the upper half. The bird skims over the water, capturing tiny animals in its bill.

The unmistakable **Brown Pelican (169)** dives for its fish food. This brown bird has a chestnut neck and white head with light yellow between the eyes.

The colorful **Red-breasted Merganser (170)** dives for fish. Mergansers have sawtoothed bills, an aid in holding slippery fish. Males have red bills, green heads, and are dark above, with brown on the belly. Females are grayish, with rufous heads.

Surf Scoters (171) are husky ducks that dive to feed on clams and mussels. Males are black with white patches on the head and bright orange-red on the bill. Females are brown.

The **American Oystercatcher (172)** moves along the mudflats at low tide, adeptly opening the shells of clams and other bivalves. Brown and white with a black head and a long bright red bill, this large shorebird is currently increasing its range northward.

Some Estuarine Fishes

The **White Perch (173)** is one of many fishes that use estuaries as spawning areas. About 1 foot long, this perch is olive-gray above, silvery green on the sides, and white on the belly. Its fins are dusky.

Sheepshead (174) are popular game fish. A big one can weigh 20 pounds. This fish is olive-green with a yellowish head and black vertical stripes.

The **Searobin (175)** is a 15-inch-long fish that "walks" on the bottom. As it creeps along, it uses the long rays of its wing-like fins to probe for crabs, mollusks, and worms. It is reddish brown with dark blotches.

The oddly named **Hogchoker (176)** is one of several flatfishes — flounders and soles — that inhabit estuaries. Its small size (6 to 8 inches) and oval shape make it easy to identify. It is slaty olive-brown with dark stripes. In spite of its name, this little fish is delicious.

The **Bluntnose Stingray (177)** is also flattened and blends in well with the bottom. Stingrays glide over sand and mud in search of worms and mollusks. Beware of stepping on or handling stingrays: there is a sharp spine at the base of the tail that can inflict a very painful wound. This ray is yellowish brown.

Sandbar Sharks (178) are one of several shark species that enter estuaries. This shark is slaty gray to brown above and white below. An adult can reach 6 feet long.

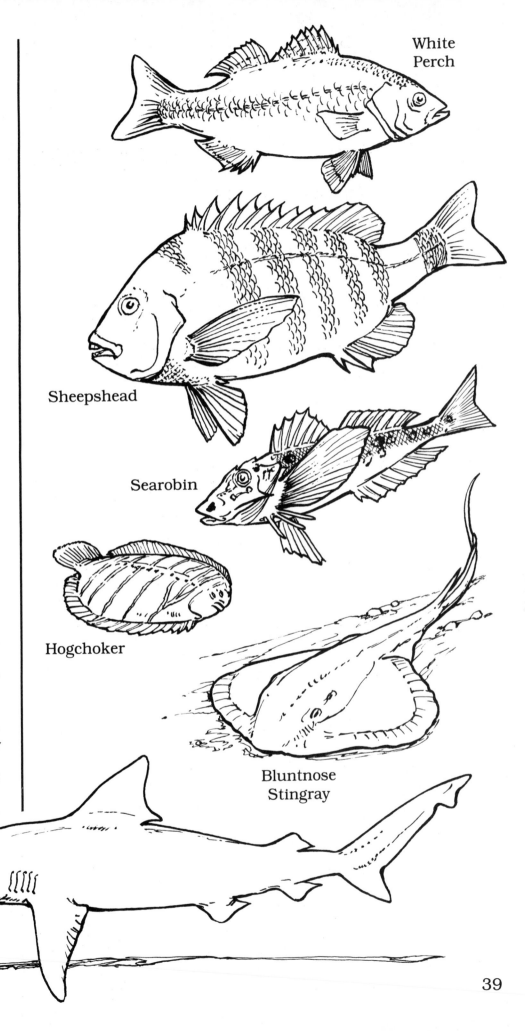

White Perch

Sheepshead

Searobin

Hogchoker

Bluntnose Stingray

Sandbar Shark

39

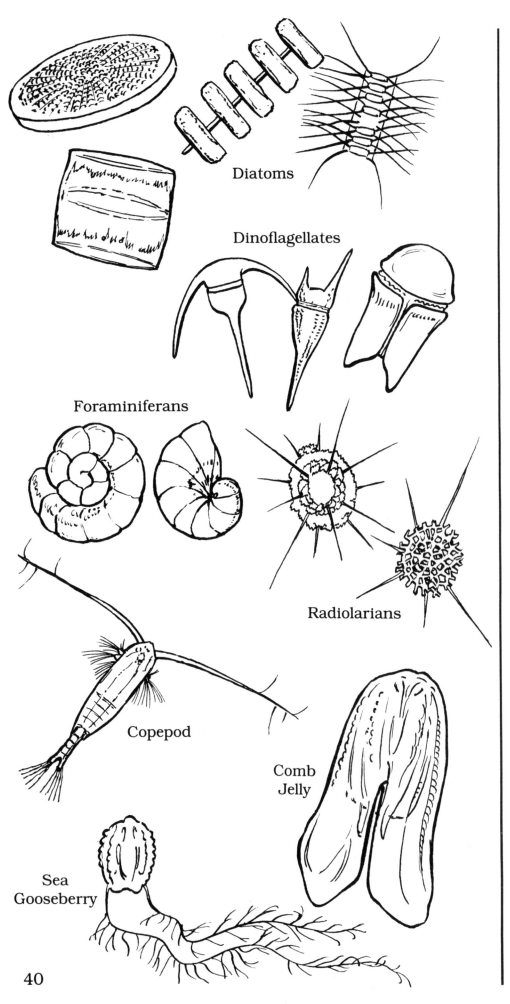

Diatoms

Dinoflagellates

Foraminiferans

Radiolarians

Copepod

Comb
Jelly

Sea
Gooseberry

Plankton

Plankton consists of tiny plants and animals that float in ocean waters, mostly at the mercy of the currents and waves. Some animals spend their entire lives as plankton. Others, such as crabs, are planktonic only during their larval stages. Plant plankton forms one of the most important bases of the oceanic food chain.

Among the plant plankton are the **diatoms (179)** and **dinoflagellates (180)**. Diatoms are single-celled plants that live in tiny "glass" shells made of silica. They are generally golden brown and may be disc-shaped, needle-like, or linked together in chains. Dinoflagellates are also single cells and tend to be golden brown. They propel themselves weakly with whip-like flagella. Some are reddish and produce a poison known as red tide. If people eat fish or shellfish that have fed upon this toxic plankton, they can become very sick.

Foraminiferans (181) and **radiolarians (182)** are tiny, one-celled animals related to amoebas. Foraminiferans make shells of chalky material that resemble tiny snail shells. Radiolarians live in glasslike shells, some of which have long spines.

Copepods (183) are tiny crustaceans. Propelled by their long antennae, copepods swim in a jerky motion. Most are transparent bluish white with a red pigment spot.

Comb jellies (184) are not jellyfish but belong to a unique group that lacks stinging cells. Comb jellies sometimes enter estuaries in large numbers. They emit their own light, like fireflies, and can make a bay glow in the dark. They are iridescent blue, red, and violet.

The **Sea Gooseberry (185)** is a comb jelly with two fringed tentacles that are used to capture animal food.

Arrowworms (186) are tiny, almost transparent predators. They attack copepods, larval fish, and anything else they can capture. They often become abundant in estuaries.

Mysid shrimp (187) reach only about one inch long but inhabit estuaries by the millions. They spend the day on the bottom but swim to the surface at night to feed. They are pale yellowish to greenish.

Horned Krill (188) are tiny shrimp barely over an inch long. They are pinkish and can occur in such vast numbers that the water is colored by them. Oceanic krill serve as an important source of food for many seabirds and large whales.

Crab larvae (189) are temporary members of the plankton. The tiny **nauplius** gradually grows and changes into a **zoea**, which has long head spines. The zoea then changes to a **megalops**, which begins to look more like a crab. These larvae are mostly translucent bluish.

The reddish **Naked Sea Butterfly (190)** is a tiny planktonic sea slug — a snail without a shell. It uses its winglike feet to help it move weakly through the sea in search of plant plankton.

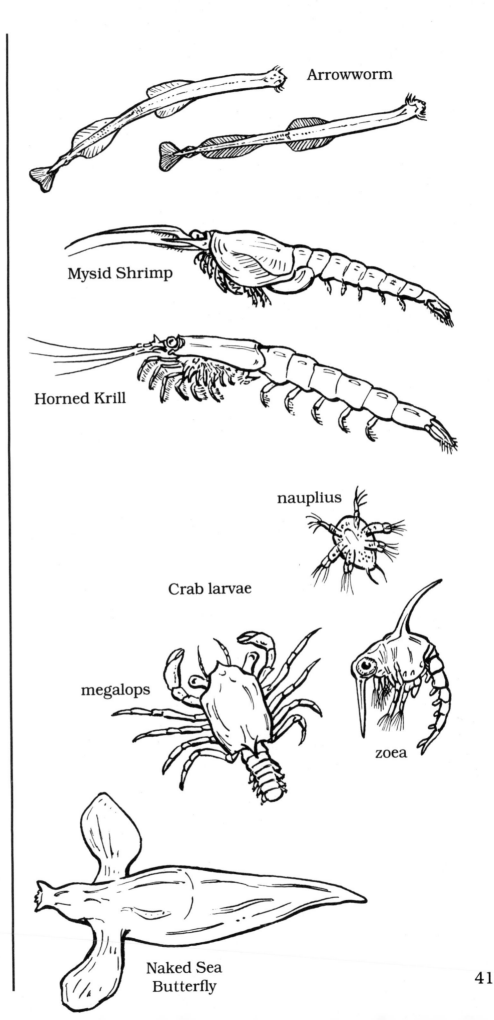

Arrowworm

Mysid Shrimp

Horned Krill

nauplius

Crab larvae

megalops

zoea

Naked Sea
Butterfly

41

Sand Dunes and Barrier Beaches

*Tidal and wave action, combined with the movement of coastal currents, piles sand up to form vast beaches and large dunes. A **barrier beach** is a long strip of dunes. It parallels the coastline and protects estuaries and salt marshes from the ravages of the sea. Beaches and dunes are unstable: the sea is constantly rearranging them during severe storms and through normal current action. Many kinds of plants have adapted to the challenge posed by life on sandy dunes. Unstable sand, severe salt spray, rapid evaporation all pose problems to which dune plants have adapted. The most hardy*

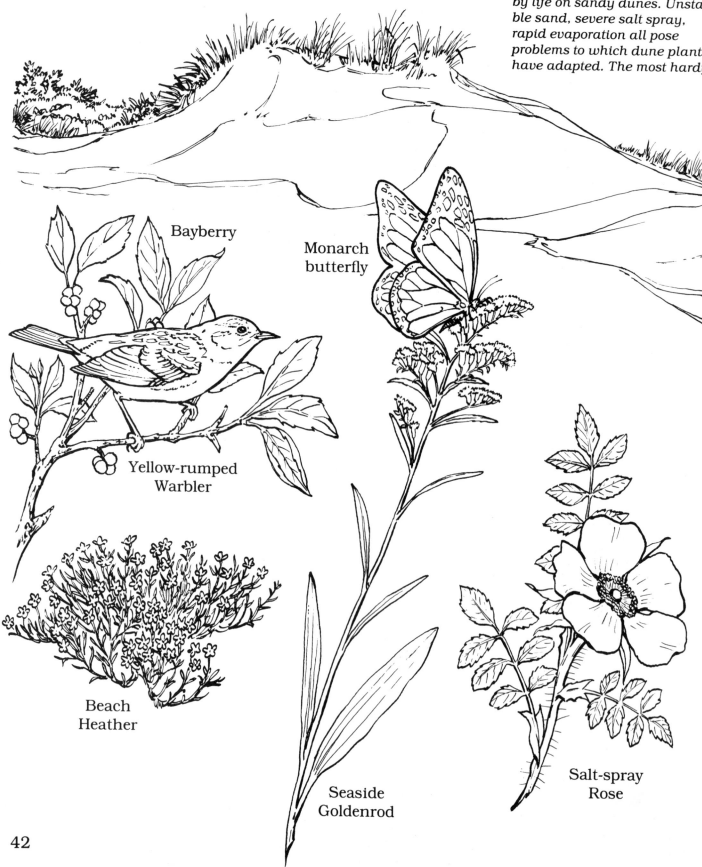

Bayberry

Monarch butterfly

Yellow-rumped Warbler

Beach Heather

Seaside Goldenrod

Salt-spray Rose

plants are found on the *fore-dunes*, the area nearest the sea. Others are found in the more protected *interdunes* and still others in the *backdunes*, the area most protected from sea spray.

Foredune plants include **Beachgrass (191)**, **Sea Rocket (192)**, and **Dusty Miller (193)**. Beachgrass has green blades and yellowish seed heads. The blades can curl up, reducing water loss by evaporation. Sea Rocket has thick, succulent leaves and pale lavender flowers that bloom throughout the summer. Dusty Miller is related to the sagebrush of western deserts. Its pale leaves are covered by tiny white hairs. It produces yellow flowers on stalks. **Beach Pea (194)** and **Salt-spray** or **Rugosa Rose (195)** may be found on the foredunes and interdunes. Beach Pea grows as a vine, its tendrils curling around other plants. Its flowers are rosy-purple. Salt-spray Rose is a dense shrub with either white or pink-red flowers. Its fruits, called rose hips, are red. **Seaside Goldenrod (196)** is common throughout the dunes and along the coast. Its succulent leaves help protect it from water loss and salt damage. Migrating **Monarch butterflies (197)** feed on the bright yellow blossoms. **Beach Heather (198)** is a grayish green plant that hugs the dunes tightly and produces small yellow flowers in summer. **Bayberry (199)** is a common shrub of interdunes and backdunes. The aromatic, greenish blue berries attract migrating swallows and **Yellow-rumped Warblers (200)**.

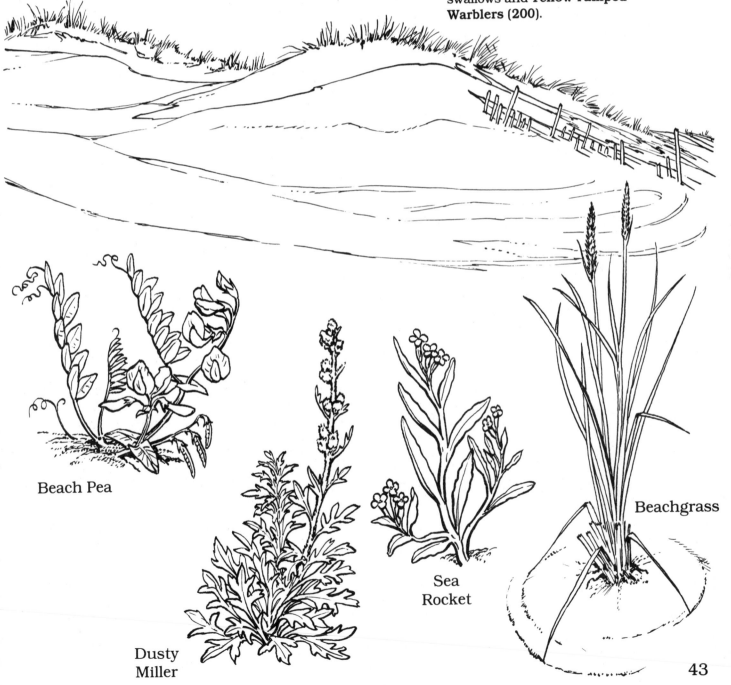

Beach Pea

Dusty
Miller

Sea
Rocket

Beachgrass

43

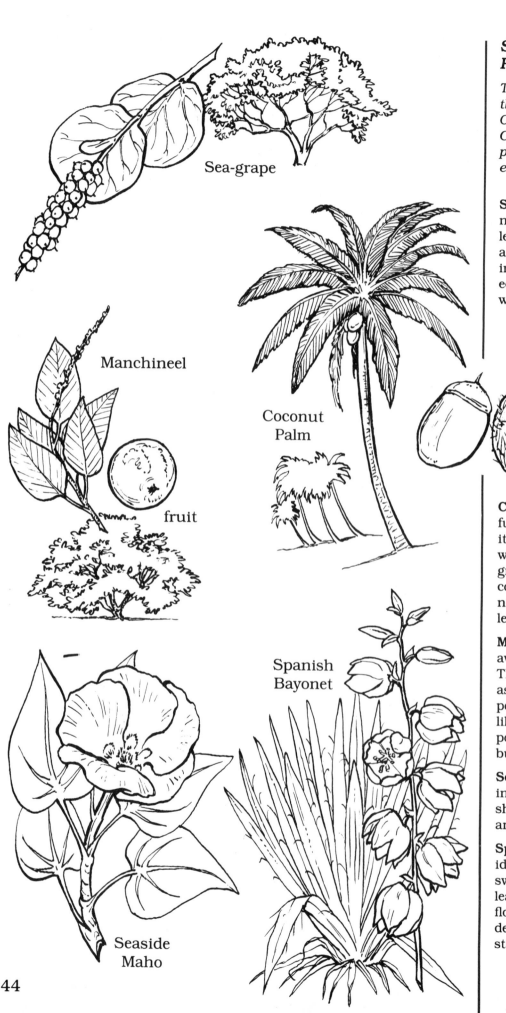

Sea-grape

Manchineel

fruit

Coconut
Palm

Spanish
Bayonet

Seaside
Maho

Southeastern Dune Plants

The beachcomber who walks the sands of the Florida and Gulf coasts as well as the Caribbean will encounter plants not found in more northern climes.

Sea-grape (201) is easily recognized by its large, leathery, oval leaves with red veins. It grows as a small rounded tree, producing clusters of green, grape-like edible fruit that turn purple when ripe.

Coconut Palm (202) is a graceful, gray-barked tree named for its unique football-sized nuts, which are green at first and gradually turn brown. The coconuts are in clusters beneath the crown of fanlike leaves.

Manchineel (203) is a tree to be avoided, especially during rain. The oval-shaped leaves, as well as the twigs and bark, drip poison when it rains. The apple-like, greenish yellow fruit is also poisonous. Look at Manchineel but from a safe distance.

Seaside Maho (204) is a spreading shrub with shiny, heart-shaped leaves. The large flowers are yellow with violet centers.

Spanish Bayonet (205) is easily identified by its rosette of thick, swordlike, sharply pointed leaves. The white, bell-shaped flowers of this yucca grow in a dense cluster atop a long central stalk.

Birds of the Dunes

Dunewalkers should look skyward in fall, as they might sight a migrating **Peregrine Falcon (206)**. This magnificent bird of prey was, like the Osprey, seriously reduced by pesticide effects. Its population is now growing well. Peregrines have sharply pointed wings and are nearly crow-sized. Adults are blue-gray above and brownish below, with a black crescent on the face.

Peregrine Falcon

Winter cold and icy winds seem little deterrent to **Snowy Owls (207)**, the white owls of the Arctic. Snowy Owls move south periodically in winter when their normal food supply, small rodents called lemmings, is too low to sustain them. Females and young birds are heavily barred with brown and black. Adult males are almost pure white.

Snowy Owls

Three small songbirds commonly associate in winter flocks on northern dunes. **Horned Larks (208)** are rufous brown above, pale below, with yellowish faces marked by a black crescent. Look for their tiny "horns," which are really feathers. **Snow Buntings (209)** look nearly all white when in flight but are rich rufous and white when on the ground. **Lapland Longspurs (210)** are streaked with blackish brown and have a chestnut collar. They are named for their long hind claw. All three species walk, not hop, over the dunes, and feed on plant seeds.

Horned Lark

Lapland Longspur

Snow Bunting

45

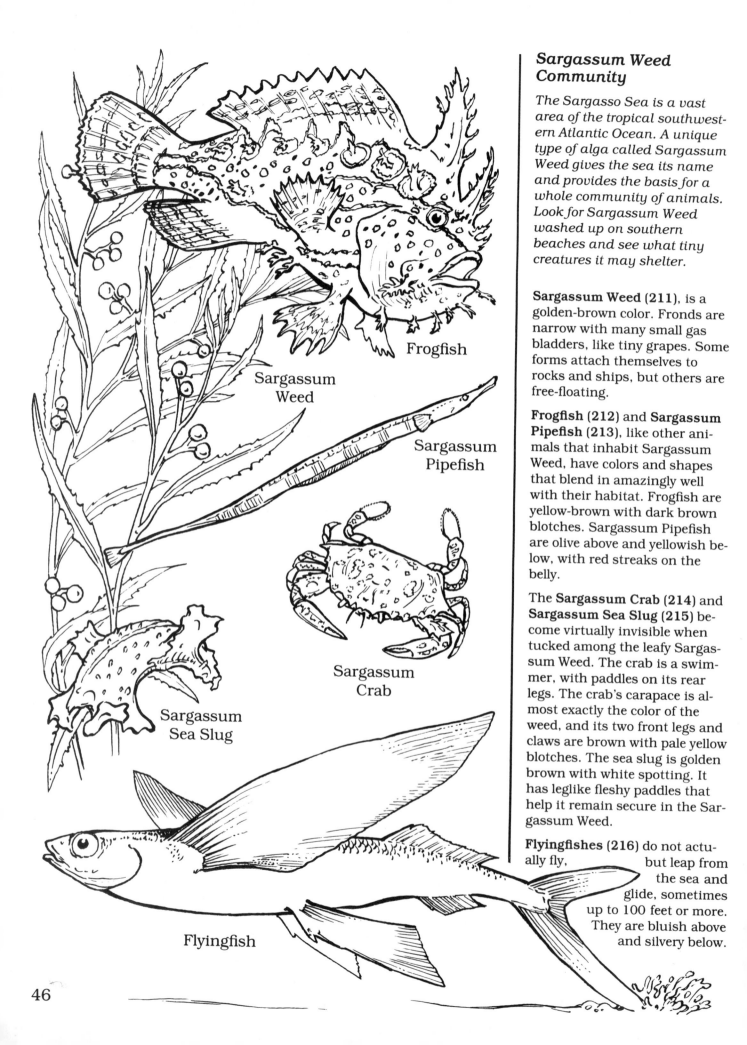

Frogfish

Sargassum Weed

Sargassum Pipefish

Sargassum Sea Slug

Sargassum Crab

Flyingfish

Sargassum Weed Community

The Sargasso Sea is a vast area of the tropical southwestern Atlantic Ocean. A unique type of alga called Sargassum Weed gives the sea its name and provides the basis for a whole community of animals. Look for Sargassum Weed washed up on southern beaches and see what tiny creatures it may shelter.

Sargassum Weed (211), is a golden-brown color. Fronds are narrow with many small gas bladders, like tiny grapes. Some forms attach themselves to rocks and ships, but others are free-floating.

Frogfish (212) and **Sargassum Pipefish (213)**, like other animals that inhabit Sargassum Weed, have colors and shapes that blend in amazingly well with their habitat. Frogfish are yellow-brown with dark brown blotches. Sargassum Pipefish are olive above and yellowish below, with red streaks on the belly.

The **Sargassum Crab (214)** and **Sargassum Sea Slug (215)** become virtually invisible when tucked among the leafy Sargassum Weed. The crab is a swimmer, with paddles on its rear legs. The crab's carapace is almost exactly the color of the weed, and its two front legs and claws are brown with pale yellow blotches. The sea slug is golden brown with white spotting. It has leglike fleshy paddles that help it remain secure in the Sargassum Weed.

Flyingfishes (216) do not actually fly, but leap from the sea and glide, sometimes up to 100 feet or more. They are bluish above and silvery below.

Porpoises and Dolphins

The names "porpoise" and "dolphin" do not mean quite the same thing. Both are types of marine mammals, but porpoises have blunt snouts and dolphins have pointed or "beaked" snouts. To further complicate matters, there is a colorful game fish, the Dolphin, that is quite distinct from the mammals of the same name.

Harbor Porpoises (217) are common from New England to Florida and along most of the Pacific Coast. Reaching about 5 feet in length, this animal is often seen swimming along the coast in groups of up to 50 individuals. Harbor Porpoises are dark brown to bluish gray, with pale gray-white sides and bellies. They feed on small fishes and squids.

Different kinds of **white-sided dolphins (218)** are found along both the Atlantic and Pacific coasts. The Atlantic species is grayish black above, with a gray and white belly and sides and a tan to yellow streak near the tail. The Pacific species is grayish on the sides and upper fin and has a pure white belly.

Bottlenose Dolphins (219) occur in warm water of both coasts. They are intelligent and are frequently exhibited doing tricks at various aquaria and seaquariums. They are almost uniformly bluish brown, with white bellies. They reach lengths of just over 10 feet.

Dolphins (220) are streamlined game fish. The males have high, rounded foreheads. Both sexes are deep blue above and brilliant yellow below, with blue spotting. The tail is yellow.

Harbor Porpoise

White-sided Dolphin

Bottlenose Dolphin

Dolphin

47

Red Mangrove

Wood Stork

White Ibis

Roseate Spoonbill

Manatee

Life Among the Mangroves

Mangroves are trees adapted to withstand high levels of saltwater. Mangrove forests and islands line the coasts of south Florida, the Florida Keys, and the Caribbean. Many glamorous birds nest among the branches of the mangroves, and diverse marine life lives on the mangrove roots.

Red Mangrove (221) has reddish roots on stilts that anchor the tree in the shifting coral sand. Leaves are a waxy, shiny green. Seedlings, called "sea pencils," look like long pods. They can float vast distances in the ocean.

Wood Storks (222), **White Ibis (223)**, and **Roseate Spoonbills (224)** all congregate in mangroves. They build their nests there, raise their young, and feed in the shallow tropical water. The Wood Stork stands over 5 feet tall and is easily recognized by its large size and bold, black-and-white plumage. The head is ashy gray with a long, downcurved bill. The White Ibis is only half the size of a Wood Stork and has black only on its wingtips. Its bill and legs are bright red. The Roseate Spoonbill is named for its spoon-shaped flattened bill, which is useful for capturing small marine animals such as worms. The face and bill are yellowish green and the wings are bright pink, especially on the shoulders. Legs are red.

The **Manatee (225)** is a large gray mammal that inhabits channels among the many mangrove islands and often enters rivers. Manatees are strict vegetarians. They eat Water Hyacinth, a nuisance plant that can clog rivers.

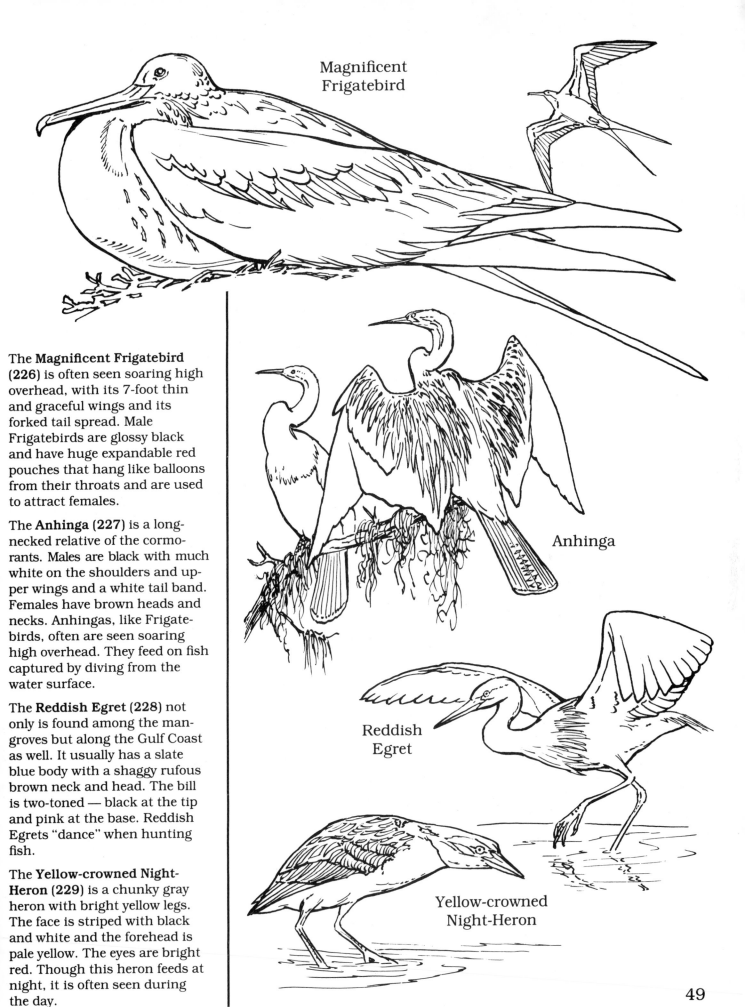

Magnificent
Frigatebird

The **Magnificent Frigatebird (226)** is often seen soaring high overhead, with its 7-foot thin and graceful wings and its forked tail spread. Male Frigatebirds are glossy black and have huge expandable red pouches that hang like balloons from their throats and are used to attract females.

The **Anhinga (227)** is a long-necked relative of the cormorants. Males are black with much white on the shoulders and upper wings and a white tail band. Females have brown heads and necks. Anhingas, like Frigatebirds, often are seen soaring high overhead. They feed on fish captured by diving from the water surface.

The **Reddish Egret (228)** not only is found among the mangroves but along the Gulf Coast as well. It usually has a slate blue body with a shaggy rufous brown neck and head. The bill is two-toned — black at the tip and pink at the base. Reddish Egrets "dance" when hunting fish.

The **Yellow-crowned Night-Heron (229)** is a chunky gray heron with bright yellow legs. The face is striped with black and white and the forehead is pale yellow. The eyes are bright red. Though this heron feeds at night, it is often seen during the day.

Anhinga

Reddish
Egret

Yellow-crowned
Night-Heron

49

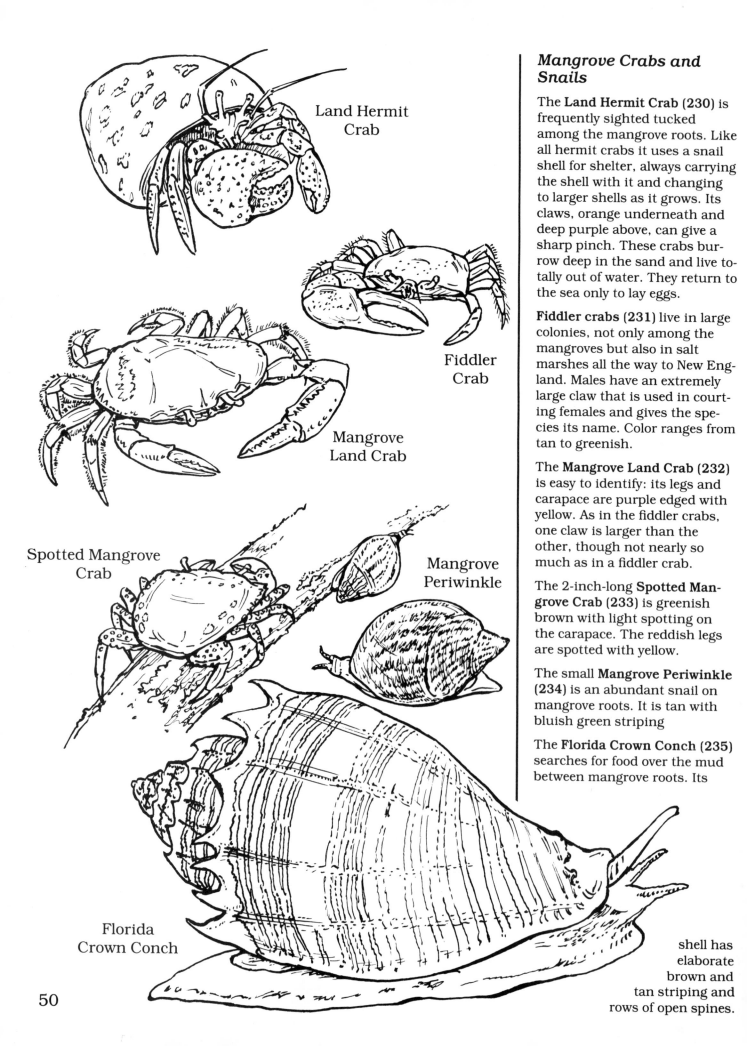

Land Hermit Crab

Fiddler Crab

Mangrove Land Crab

Spotted Mangrove Crab

Mangrove Periwinkle

Florida Crown Conch

Mangrove Crabs and Snails

The **Land Hermit Crab (230)** is frequently sighted tucked among the mangrove roots. Like all hermit crabs it uses a snail shell for shelter, always carrying the shell with it and changing to larger shells as it grows. Its claws, orange underneath and deep purple above, can give a sharp pinch. These crabs burrow deep in the sand and live totally out of water. They return to the sea only to lay eggs.

Fiddler crabs (231) live in large colonies, not only among the mangroves but also in salt marshes all the way to New England. Males have an extremely large claw that is used in courting females and gives the species its name. Color ranges from tan to greenish.

The **Mangrove Land Crab (232)** is easy to identify: its legs and carapace are purple edged with yellow. As in the fiddler crabs, one claw is larger than the other, though not nearly so much as in a fiddler crab.

The 2-inch-long **Spotted Mangrove Crab (233)** is greenish brown with light spotting on the carapace. The reddish legs are spotted with yellow.

The small **Mangrove Periwinkle (234)** is an abundant snail on mangrove roots. It is tan with bluish green striping

The **Florida Crown Conch (235)** searches for food over the mud between mangrove roots. Its shell has elaborate brown and tan striping and rows of open spines.

50

Animals of the Mangrove Prop Roots

Tunicates of many kinds grow like clusters of colorful grapes on the roots. These baglike animals filter the warm water, capturing tiny prey in their mucus-lined gills. The one-inch-long **Mangrove Tunicate (236)** is reddish orange. Clusters are attached to roots by vine-like structures called stolons. The delicate **Painted Tunicate (237)** is pale pink with a purple band around the openings where water enters and leaves.

Crozier's Flatworm (238) is often seen feeding on clusters of tunicates. It is tan with wavy brown lines.

The **Red-banded Fanworm (239)** is a segmented worm that is recognized by its broad, fan-like appendages, which give the worm its popular name, the "feather-duster worm." The animal lives in a tough fibrous tube that it constructs. Only its head emerges to fan the water and capture prey.

Groups of purplish **Flat Tree Oysters (240)** often cover whole sections of mangrove roots. Like the tunicates, they are permanently attached and filter their food from the currents.

Looking like a tentacled mass of jelly, the 3-inch-long **Collared Sand Anemone (241)** is common in the sand among the mangrove roots. It is greenish with white banding.

Juvenile **Sergeant Majors (242),** yellowish with black bands, and **Schoolmasters (243),** pale yellow with yellow fins, snap at tiny plankton among the mangrove roots.

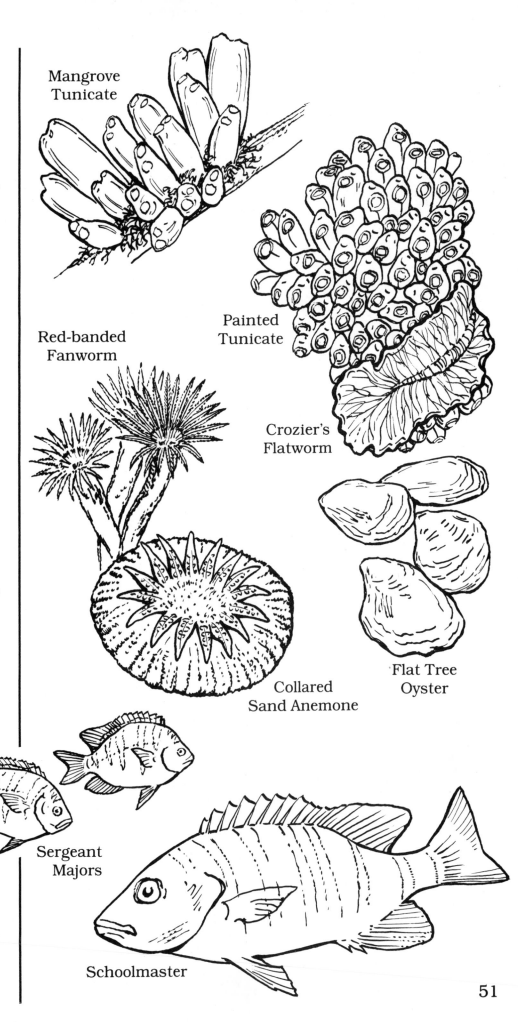

Mangrove Tunicate

Painted Tunicate

Red-banded Fanworm

Crozier's Flatworm

Collared Sand Anemone

Flat Tree Oyster

Sergeant Majors

Schoolmaster

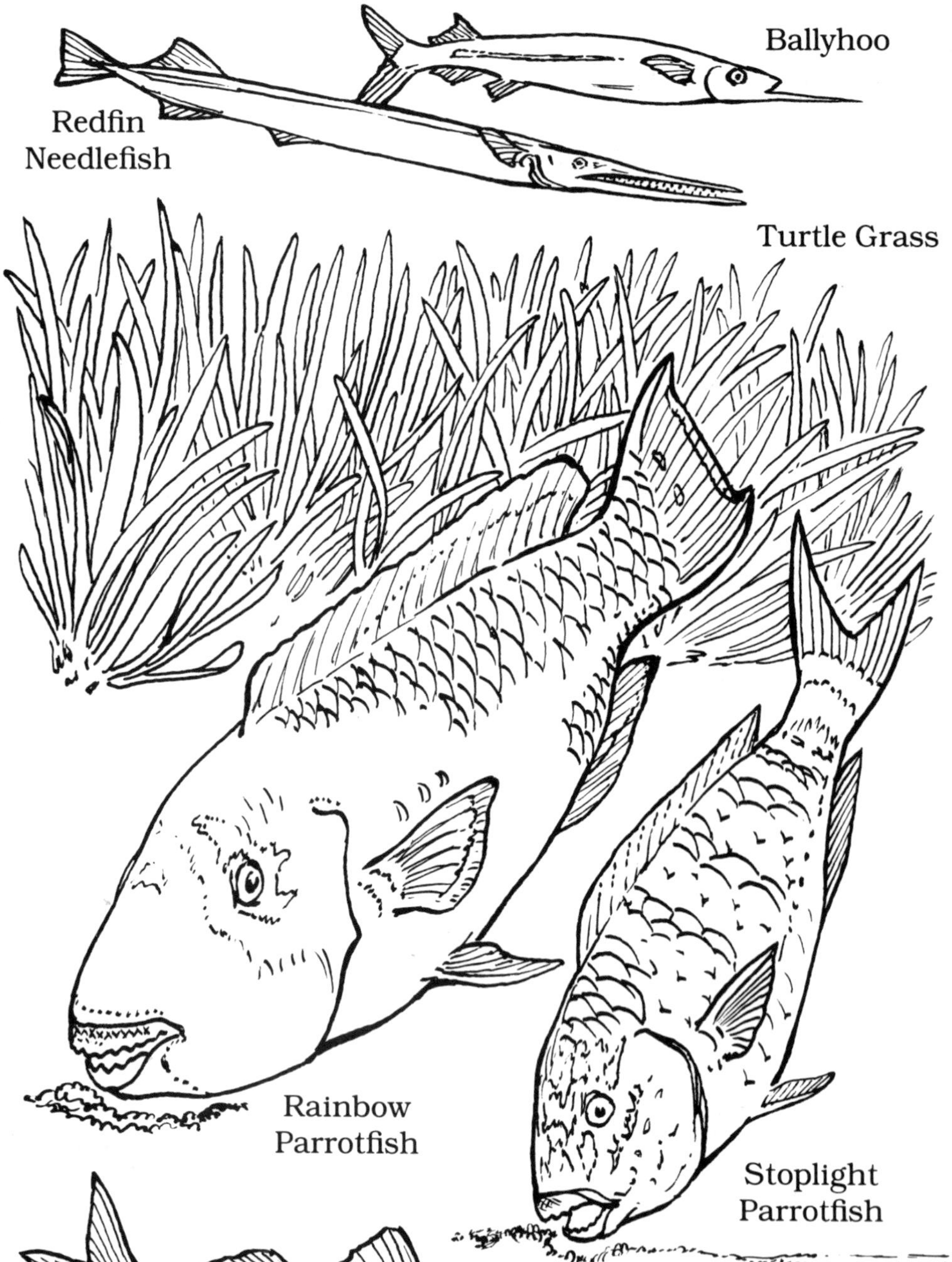

Ballyhoo

Redfin
Needlefish

Turtle Grass

Rainbow
Parrotfish

Stoplight
Parrotfish

Spotted
Goatfish

French
Grunt

Cushion
Sea Star

Long-spined
Black Urchin

Turtle Grass Meadows

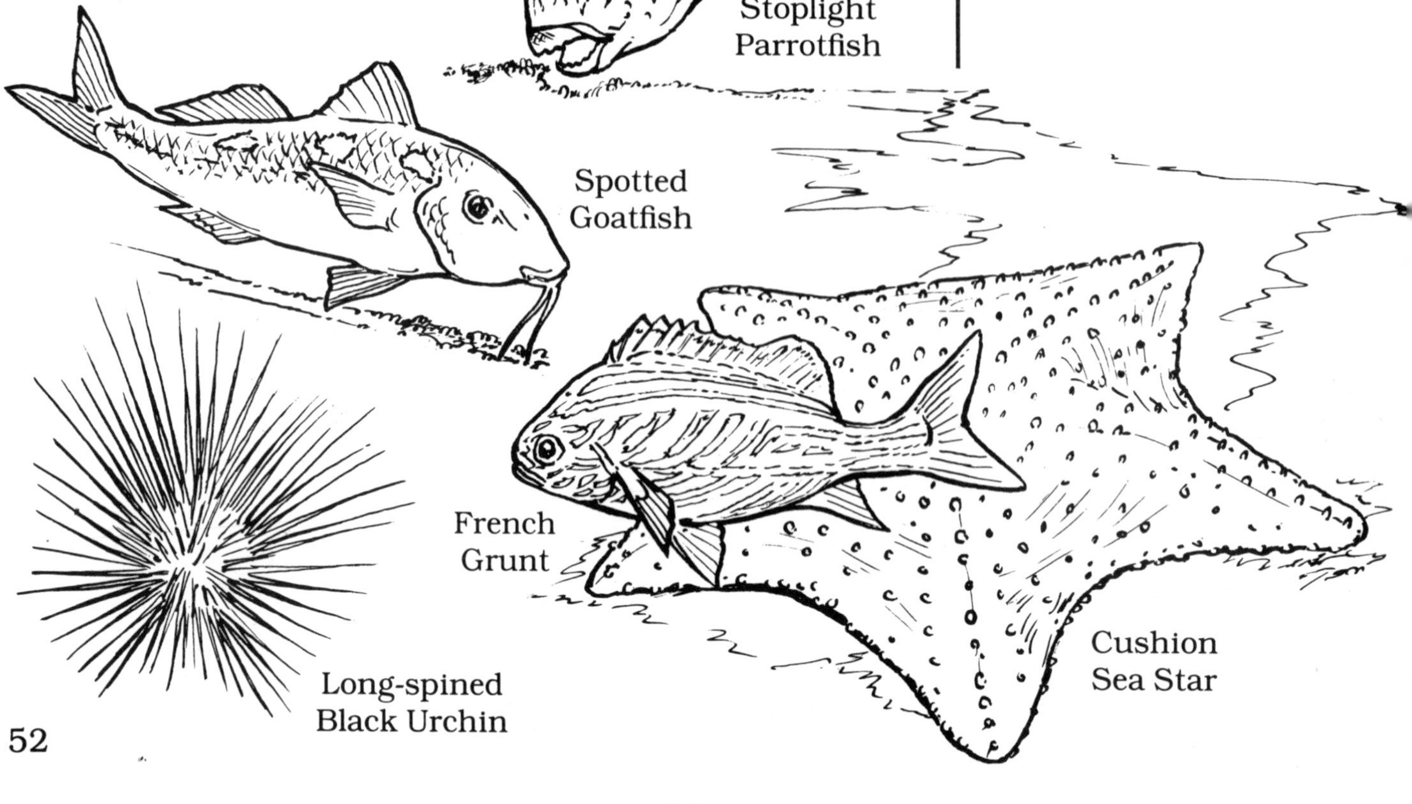

Turtle Grass (244) is a marine grass that grows on warm coral sands protected by coral reef. Many species, including sea turtles such as the **Hawksbill Turtle (245)**, enjoy the food and protection afforded by these unique undersea meadows. Schools of **parrotfish**, such as the **Stoplight Parrotfish (246)** and the **Rainbow Parrotfish (247)**, graze like finned cattle on the coral sand. The sound of their crunching, somewhat like static on a radio, is easily audible to the snorkeler. Stoplight Parrotfish are speckled black with red fins and bellies, but a few males become brilliant turquoise with yellow spotting. Rainbow Parrotfish are tan and pale green. Some males become very large. Schools of blue- and yellow-striped **French Grunts (248)** share the Turtle Grass with the parrotfish. Grunts, like many other fishes, can make an audible sound with their swim bladders, hence the name "grunt." Probing among the sand grains with a thin tentacle from its lower jaw, the **Spotted Goatfish (249)** is seeking tiny worms and other food items. At the water's surface swim the slender **Redfin Needlefish (250)** and **Ballyhoo (251)**, quickly snapping up tiny planktonic animals in their needle-like jaws. The delicate, brilliantly colored juvenile **Cocoa Damselfish (252)** lives in abandoned shells of **Queen Conchs (253)**. This little iridescent purple and yellow fish will retreat quickly to its shell when threatened. When wading among Turtle Grass, keep an eye out for the **Long-spined Black Urchin (254)**. Its spines are poisonous and painfully sharp, like the stinger of a wasp. Another fearsome creature of the Turtle Grass is the **Great Barracuda (255)**, a sleek, silvery blue fish that can reach lengths of 3 feet but is usually smaller. This fish looks dangerous but rarely attacks humans. In contrast to the bold and active barracudas, the **Donkey Dung Sea Cucumber (256)** and the **Cushion Sea Star (257)** look utterly peaceful as they rest in the coral sand among the Turtle Grass. The sea cucumber is pale brownish above, with a bright orange-red belly. The sea star is reddish orange.

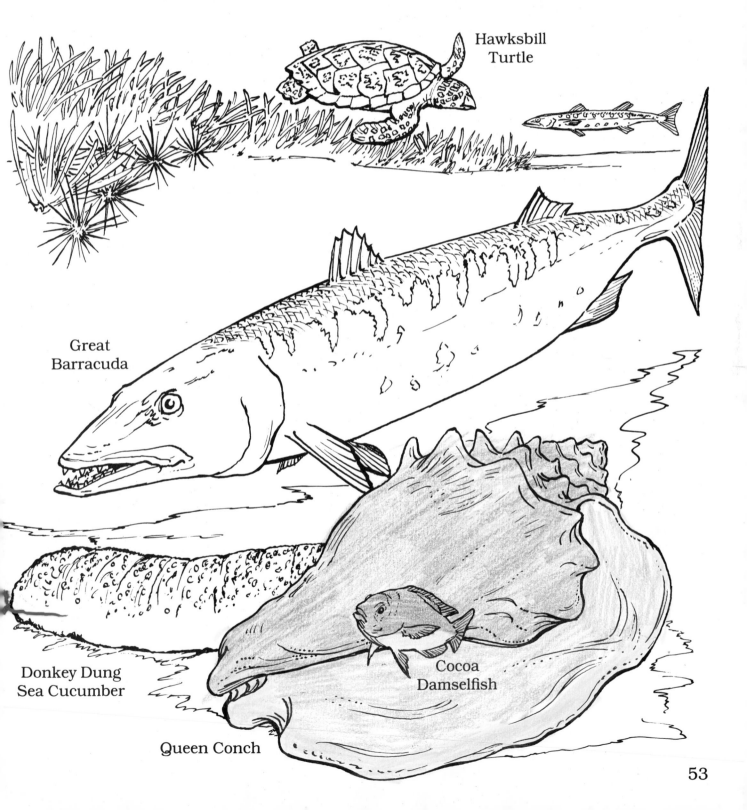

Hawksbill Turtle

Great Barracuda

Donkey Dung Sea Cucumber

Cocoa Damselfish

Queen Conch

Elkhorn Coral

Staghorn Coral

Boulder Coral

Rose Coral

Red Coral

Brain Coral

The Coral Reef

Corals live in warm tropical waters. They are tiny animals related to sea anemones. Like tiny anemones, most corals capture plankton with stinging cells in their ring of tentacles. Coral animals secrete calcium carbonate, a hard rocky material in which the coral animals are embedded. When the coral animals die, their "skeletons" remain, forming the bases of vast colonies called reefs. The reefs serve as habitat for vast numbers of colorful fishes and invertebrates. Reef waters are normally very clear. The best way to see the rich life of the reef is to snorkel leisurely at the surface.

Staghorn and **Elkhorn corals** have many branches and grow in shallow water. Staghorns (**258**) are white or tan, with multitudes of thin branches. Elkhorns (**259**) are yellow or tan with wide, flattened branches.

Boulder Coral (260) is rounded and may be 5 feet in diameter. Usually greenish, it is abundant throughout the Caribbean.

Rose Coral (261) is named for its resemblance to the flower. It is yellow, with wavy edges, and is only about 3 inches long. Look for it while snorkeling over beds of Turtle Grass.

Red Coral (262) is bright red or orange. The coral animals, called polyps, are yellow and, like many corals, are active mostly at night.

Brain Coral (263) has wavy grooves, like the surface of a human brain. Some brain corals are quite large. Color varies — this coral may be greenish, yellowish, or brownish.

Fire Coral (264) is not a true coral but is related to the dangerous Portuguese Man-of-War. Widely branched, Fire Coral is yellowish tan with pale tips. If you brush against it, you will feel a stinging sensation.

The **Fireworm (265)**, like Fire Coral, can produce a highly irritating sting if touched. This colorful greenish worm with red bristles is common on reefs.

The **Tan Bushy Soft Coral (266)** is a true coral but sways softly in the currents, looking more like a shrub than an animal colony. Often resting vertically among the coral branches

are **Trumpetfish (267)**. These elongate fish can change color but are usually tan or rich brown with blue spots.

Sea fans (268) are wide soft corals that have a fanlike latticework. Some are deep violet. A small colorful snail, the **Flamingo Tongue (269)**, lives on sea fans and soft corals, feeding on them.

Sponges of many colors can be found on the reef. The **Giant Tube Sponge (270)** looks like a cluster of long (up to 3 feet), bluish or reddish cylinders. The **Strawberry Sponge (271)** is rounded, with bumps on the surface. It is deep red. The **Iridescent Tube Sponge (272)** is quite convoluted and is a shimmering silvery blue color.

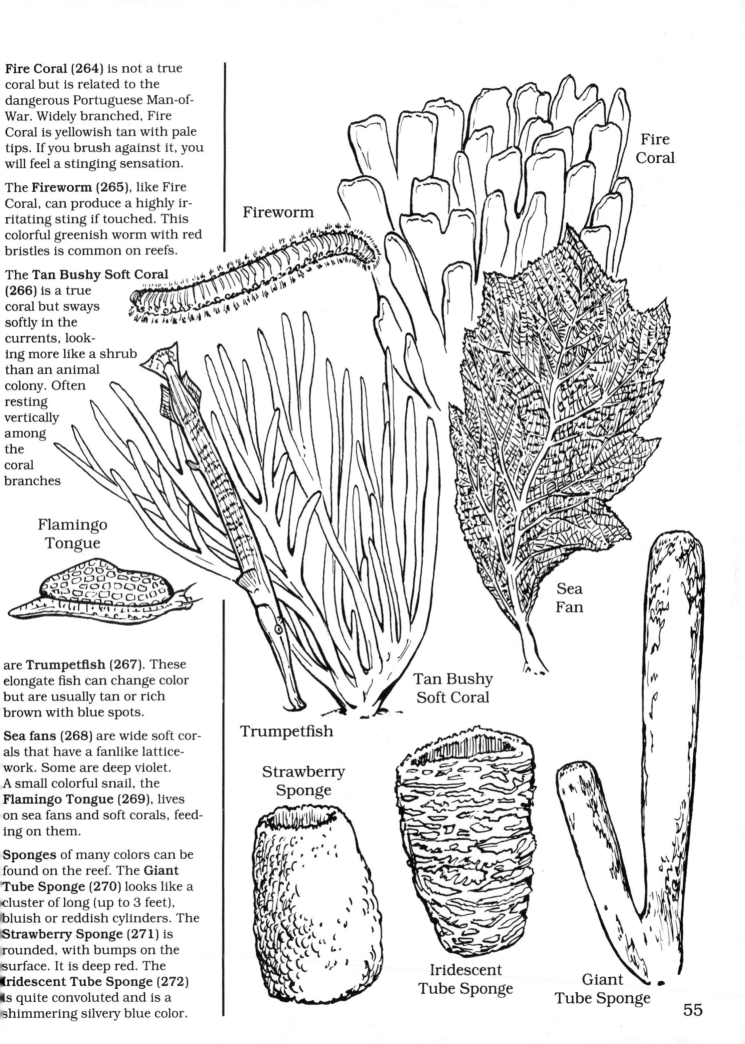

Fire Coral

Fireworm

Sea Fan

Tan Bushy Soft Coral

Flamingo Tongue

Trumpetfish

Strawberry Sponge

Iridescent Tube Sponge

Giant Tube Sponge

55

Queen
Angelfish

Rock
Beauty

Spotfin
Butterflyfish

Blue
Tang

Porkfish

Queen
Triggerfish

Squirrelfish

Spanish
Hogfish

Animals of the Reef

Angelfishes are rather disklike in shape, with long tapering fins. The **Queen Angelfish (273)** is yellow mixed with blue, with a black "crown" atop the head. The **Rock Beauty (274)** is deep yellow with black sides.

Butterflyfishes are related to angelfishes and are equally brilliant in color. The **Spotfin Butterflyfish (275)** is white and yellow with a bold black spot near its tail and a black line through its eye.

Porkfish (276) and **Blue Tang (277)** are often found in large schools swimming among the corals. Porkfish are striped with pale blue and yellow, with two black stripes. Tang are deep blue as adults but bright yellow when young. Tang have a sharp spine at the base of the tail that is used in defense.

The **Queen Triggerfish (278)** also has a spine, but it is on top of the fish's head rather than near its tail. This long-snouted fish can feed on sea urchins by poking its narrow mouth between the sharp spines. Color varies but is a mixture of blue and yellow.

The **Spanish Hogfish (279)** also has a sloping head, which helps it poke between coral crevices. Adults are mostly yellow, with blue or sometimes red on their upper sides.

Squirrelfishes (280) are silvery red. Most spend the day tucked in among the coral heads, emerging to feed at night. They have huge black eyes.

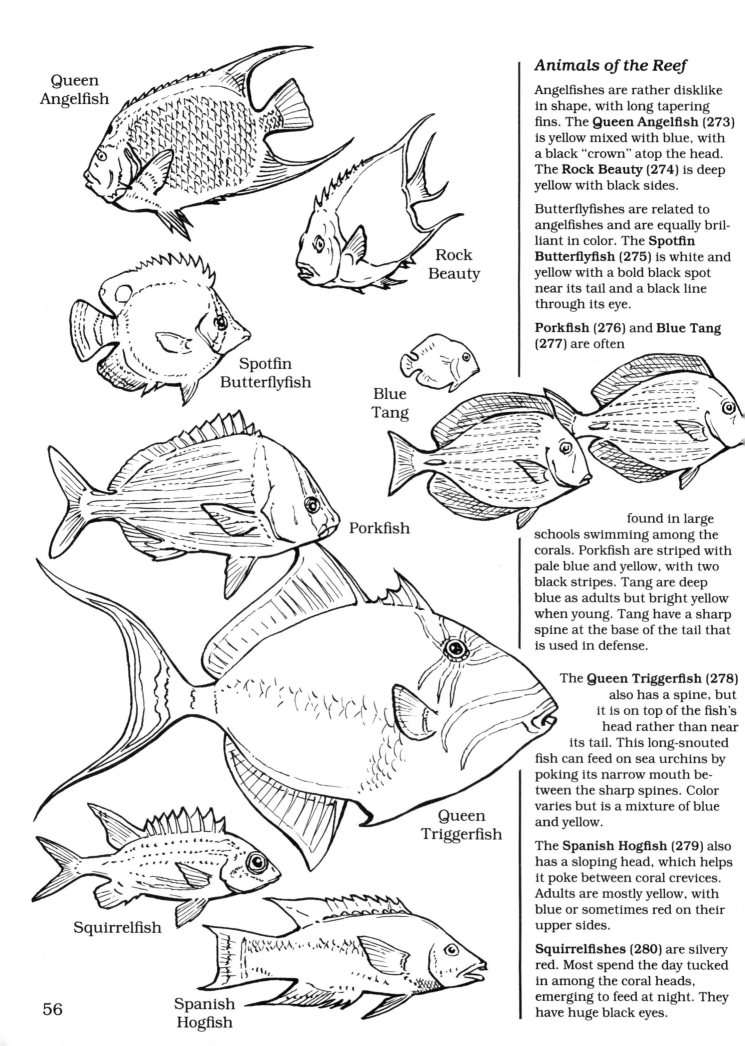

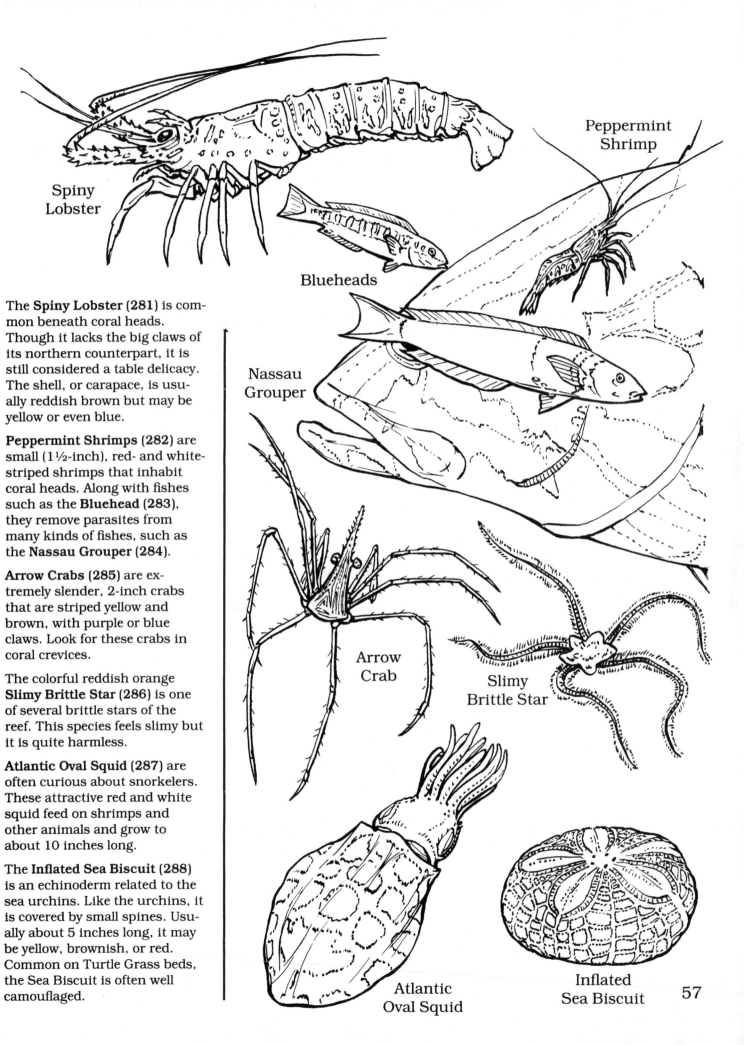

Spiny
Lobster

Peppermint
Shrimp

Blueheads

Nassau
Grouper

The **Spiny Lobster (281)** is common beneath coral heads. Though it lacks the big claws of its northern counterpart, it is still considered a table delicacy. The shell, or carapace, is usually reddish brown but may be yellow or even blue.

Peppermint Shrimps (282) are small (1½-inch), red- and white-striped shrimps that inhabit coral heads. Along with fishes such as the **Bluehead (283)**, they remove parasites from many kinds of fishes, such as the **Nassau Grouper (284)**.

Arrow Crabs (285) are extremely slender, 2-inch crabs that are striped yellow and brown, with purple or blue claws. Look for these crabs in coral crevices.

The colorful reddish orange **Slimy Brittle Star (286)** is one of several brittle stars of the reef. This species feels slimy but it is quite harmless.

Atlantic Oval Squid (287) are often curious about snorkelers. These attractive red and white squid feed on shrimps and other animals and grow to about 10 inches long.

The **Inflated Sea Biscuit (288)** is an echinoderm related to the sea urchins. Like the urchins, it is covered by small spines. Usually about 5 inches long, it may be yellow, brownish, or red. Common on Turtle Grass beds, the Sea Biscuit is often well camouflaged.

Arrow
Crab

Slimy
Brittle Star

Atlantic
Oval Squid

Inflated
Sea Biscuit

57

Pacific Coast Seashores

From the Baja Peninsula northward through California, Oregon, and Washington, West Coast seashores offer rich diversity and unique creatures. Among the mammals are the **California Sea Lion**, the **Elephant Seal**, and the **Sea Otter**. Sea lions differ from seals in that they have small external ears, visible at close range. They also have longer necks and characteristically sit upright, resembling dogs with flippers. The California Sea Lion (**289**) lives colonially all along the Pacific Coast. Males weigh up to four times more than females (up to 660 pounds) and their

barking can often be heard even at a considerable distance. Sea lions are buffy brown. The huge Elephant Seal (**290**) is recognized by the large drooping snout found on the adult males. The snout, which gives the animal its name, is inflated during mating season. An adult male can weigh 3½ tons. These seals are less common than sea lions but also occur all along the Pacific Coast, usually on offshore islands. Elephant Seals are grayish brown, tan below.

The Sea Otter (**291**), once threatened with extinction, is now common along the northern Pacific Coast, where it feeds on sea urchins, mollusks, and fish that inhabit kelp beds. Sea Otters rarely come on land. They prefer to feed while floating on their backs, using a rock to crack open a mollusk or sea urchin. They are dark brown with a yellowish tan head and neck.

Tufted
Puffin

Heermann's
Gull

Black
Oystercatcher

Among the many bird species of the western coast, look for the **Black Oystercatcher (292)**, the **Black Turnstone (293)**, and the **Wandering Tattler (294)** as they probe among the rocks in the intertidal zone. Each bird is dark and well camouflaged against a background of black rocks and dark kelp. The slate gray **Heermann's Gull (295)**, also common along rocky inter-

tidal areas, has a white head and bright red bill. Offshore islands are nesting sites for the colorful **Tufted Puffin (296)**. The puffin's body is sleek black,

its feet bright orange, and its bill is reddish orange. The white face is set off by a plume of light yellow feathers.

Elephant
Seal

Sea
Otter

California
Sea Lion

Wandering
Tattler

Black
Turnstone

59

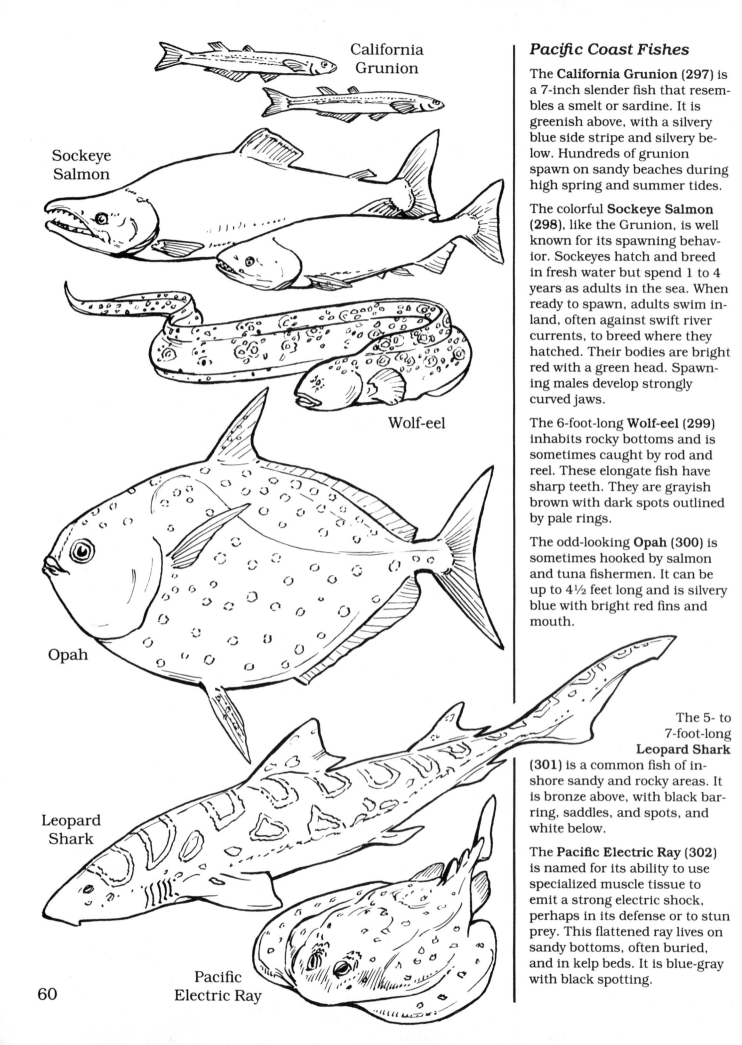

California Grunion

Sockeye Salmon

Wolf-eel

Opah

Leopard Shark

Pacific Electric Ray

Pacific Coast Fishes

The **California Grunion (297)** is a 7-inch slender fish that resembles a smelt or sardine. It is greenish above, with a silvery blue side stripe and silvery below. Hundreds of grunion spawn on sandy beaches during high spring and summer tides.

The colorful **Sockeye Salmon (298)**, like the Grunion, is well known for its spawning behavior. Sockeyes hatch and breed in fresh water but spend 1 to 4 years as adults in the sea. When ready to spawn, adults swim inland, often against swift river currents, to breed where they hatched. Their bodies are bright red with a green head. Spawning males develop strongly curved jaws.

The 6-foot-long **Wolf-eel (299)** inhabits rocky bottoms and is sometimes caught by rod and reel. These elongate fish have sharp teeth. They are grayish brown with dark spots outlined by pale rings.

The odd-looking **Opah (300)** is sometimes hooked by salmon and tuna fishermen. It can be up to 4½ feet long and is silvery blue with bright red fins and mouth.

The 5- to 7-foot-long **Leopard Shark (301)** is a common fish of inshore sandy and rocky areas. It is bronze above, with black barring, saddles, and spots, and white below.

The **Pacific Electric Ray (302)** is named for its ability to use specialized muscle tissue to emit a strong electric shock, perhaps in its defense or to stun prey. This flattened ray lives on sandy bottoms, often buried, and in kelp beds. It is blue-gray with black spotting.

60

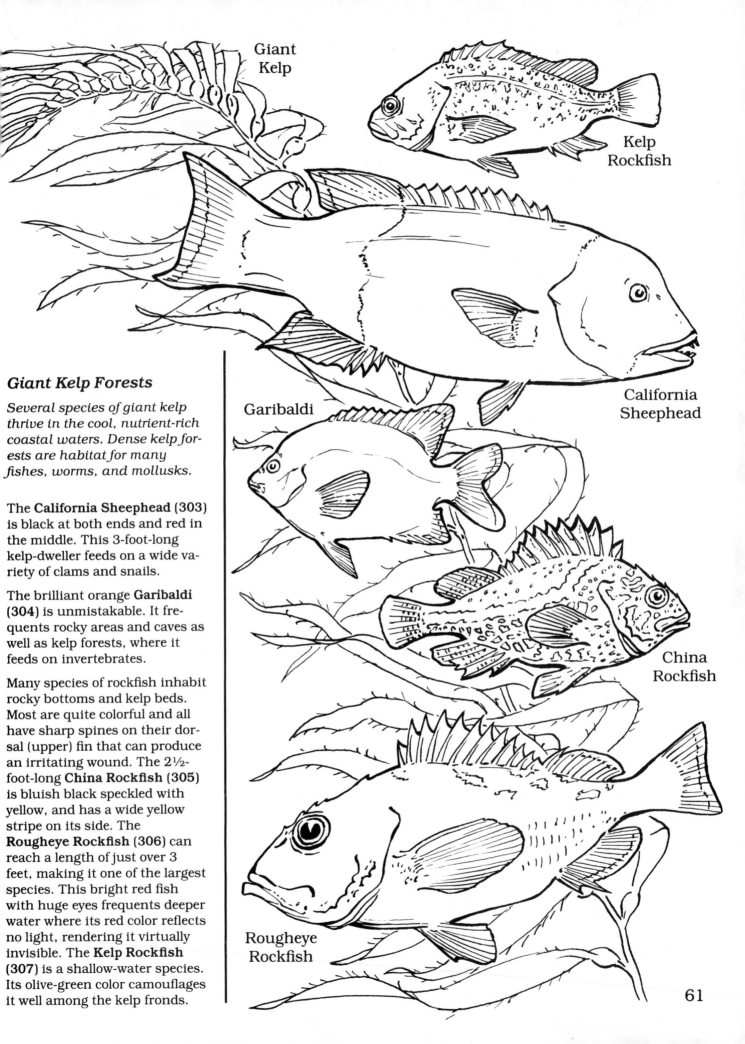

Giant
Kelp

Kelp
Rockfish

Giant Kelp Forests

Several species of giant kelp thrive in the cool, nutrient-rich coastal waters. Dense kelp forests are habitat for many fishes, worms, and mollusks.

The **California Sheephead (303)** is black at both ends and red in the middle. This 3-foot-long kelp-dweller feeds on a wide variety of clams and snails.

The brilliant orange **Garibaldi (304)** is unmistakable. It frequents rocky areas and caves as well as kelp forests, where it feeds on invertebrates.

Many species of rockfish inhabit rocky bottoms and kelp beds. Most are quite colorful and all have sharp spines on their dorsal (upper) fin that can produce an irritating wound. The 2½-foot-long **China Rockfish (305)** is bluish black speckled with yellow, and has a wide yellow stripe on its side. The **Rougheye Rockfish (306)** can reach a length of just over 3 feet, making it one of the largest species. This bright red fish with huge eyes frequents deeper water where its red color reflects no light, rendering it virtually invisible. The **Kelp Rockfish (307)** is a shallow-water species. Its olive-green color camouflages it well among the kelp fronds.

Garibaldi

California
Sheephead

China
Rockfish

Rougheye
Rockfish

61

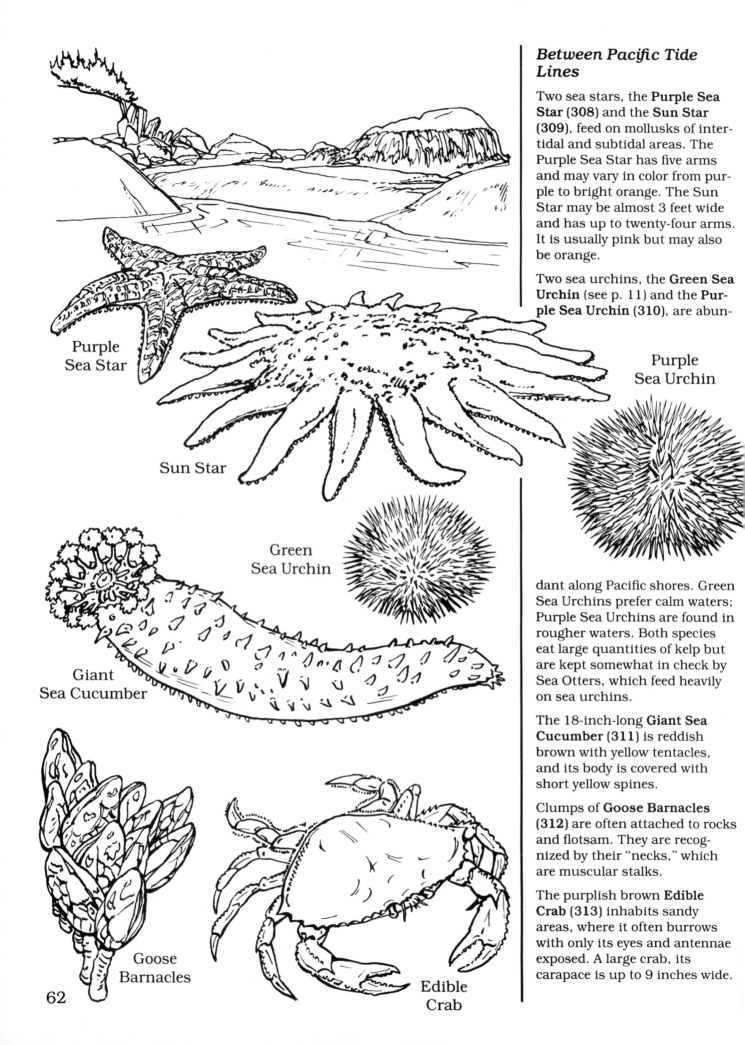

Between Pacific Tide Lines

Two sea stars, the **Purple Sea Star (308)** and the **Sun Star (309)**, feed on mollusks of intertidal and subtidal areas. The Purple Sea Star has five arms and may vary in color from purple to bright orange. The Sun Star may be almost 3 feet wide and has up to twenty-four arms. It is usually pink but may also be orange.

Two sea urchins, the **Green Sea Urchin** (see p. 11) and the **Purple Sea Urchin (310)**, are abun-

dant along Pacific shores. Green Sea Urchins prefer calm waters; Purple Sea Urchins are found in rougher waters. Both species eat large quantities of kelp but are kept somewhat in check by Sea Otters, which feed heavily on sea urchins.

The 18-inch-long **Giant Sea Cucumber (311)** is reddish brown with yellow tentacles, and its body is covered with short yellow spines.

Clumps of **Goose Barnacles (312)** are often attached to rocks and flotsam. They are recognized by their "necks," which are muscular stalks.

The purplish brown **Edible Crab (313)** inhabits sandy areas, where it often burrows with only its eyes and antennae exposed. A large crab, its carapace is up to 9 inches wide.

Purple Sea Star

Sun Star

Purple Sea Urchin

Green Sea Urchin

Giant Sea Cucumber

Goose Barnacles

Edible Crab

The beautiful **Green Sea Anemone** (314) is common in tidepools. It is deep turquoise green.

The **Sea Pen** (315) is related to sea anemones. Large colonies frequent sandy waters below the tide line. Sea pens, which are colored pale orange, feed on tiny planktonic animals.

Chitons are mollusks that are covered by a series of eight plate-like shells. The **Lined Red Chiton** (316) is 1½ inches long; it is colored orange-red with wavy black lines. The **Giant Pacific Chiton** (317) can reach one foot in length. Its eight armored plates are normally covered by an orange-red girdle.

Abalones are an odd family of large snails found along the Pacific Coast. They are known for their delicious flavor. Their shells are flattened, with four to six holes for venting water and waste material. They cling tightly to rocks, mostly feeding on kelp. The inside of their shells is multicolored iridescent. The **Pink Abalone** (318) has a wavy shell that is mostly pinkish red inside.

An octopus has eight tentacles, each lined with two rows of suckers. Octopuses feed on crabs, clams, and snails, all of which they crack with their sharp, birdlike beaks. The **Pacific Octopus** (319) is usually dark reddish, with arms 2 to 3 feet long, though some large individuals can grow arms up to 14 feet long.

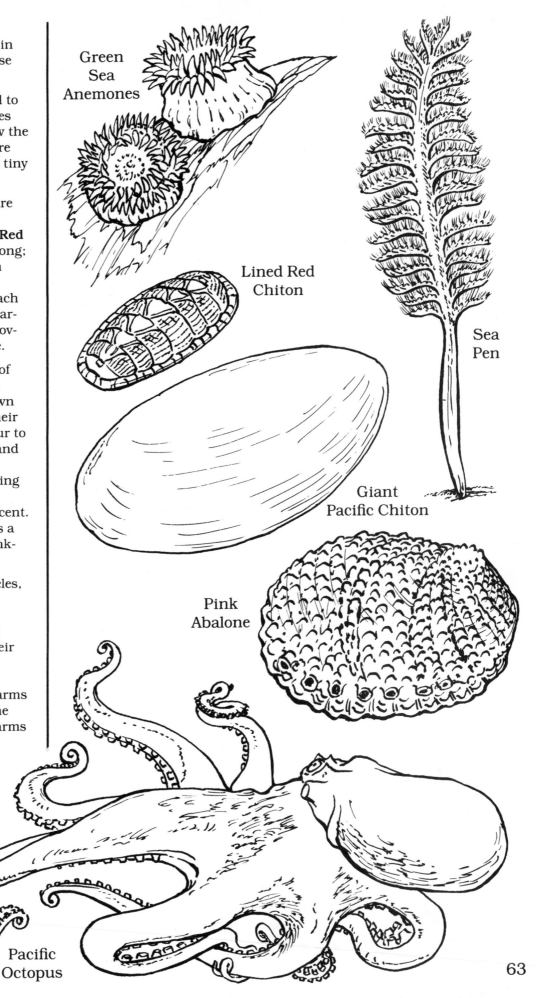

Green Sea Anemones

Sea Pen

Lined Red Chiton

Giant Pacific Chiton

Pink Abalone

Pacific Octopus

63

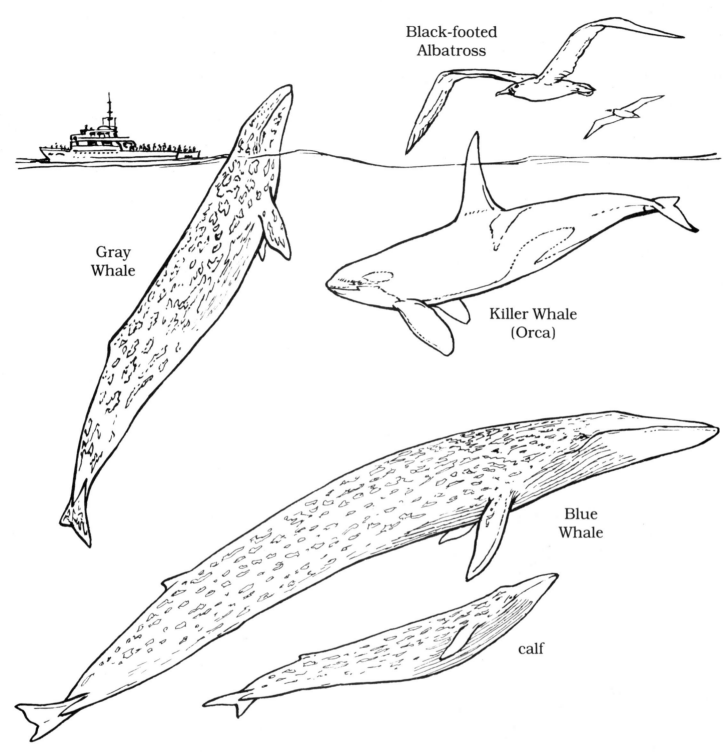

Black-footed
Albatross

Gray
Whale

Killer Whale
(Orca)

Blue
Whale

calf

Off Pacific Shores

A day on a boat offshore from Santa Barbara, San Francisco, or Vancouver can bring you close to some of the earth's most magnificent animals. From November through May, you may encounter groups (called pods) of **Gray Whales (320)** migrating between their summer feeding area in the plankton-rich northern seas and their breeding grounds in lagoons off Baja California and Mexico. These whales, 45 feet in length, are mottled gray. The world's largest animal is the **Blue Whale (321)**, which, like the Gray Whale, has also begun to rebound under protection. A fully grown female may be 100 feet in length and weigh up to 160 tons! A newborn calf is over 20 feet long. These immense animals feed on tiny shrimplike krill (see p. 41). Packs of **Killer Whales**, or **Orcas (322)**, occasionally prey on other whales but more commonly feed on fishes, seals, sea lions, and sea turtles. Orcas are strikingly patterned in black and white. A fully grown male may be 35 feet in length. Often gliding gracefully at the water's surface, close to feeding whales, the **Black-footed Albatross (323)** has a wingspan of nearly 7 feet. It is rich brown with white at the base of the bill.

144

151

152

153

154

45

146

148

147

149

150

155

156

157

158

159

160

161

162

163

164

165

166

167

168

69

170

171

172

173

174

175

176

177

178

179

180

181

182

183

184

185

186

187

188

189

190

191

192

193

94

197

200

199

198

196

195

201

202

203

204

205

206

207

208

209

210

211

212

213

214

215

216